Classical Heritage and European Identities

T0316363

Classical Heritage and European Identities examines how the heritages of classical antiquity have been used to construct European identities, and especially the concept of citizenship, in Denmark from the eighteenth century to the present day. It implements a critical historiographical perspective in line with recent work on the "reception" of classical antiquity that has stressed the dialectic relationship between past, present and future.

Arguing that the continuous employment and appropriation of classical heritages in the Danish context constitute an interesting case of an imagined geography that is simultaneously based on both national and European identities, this book shows how Denmark's imagined geography is naturalised through very distinctive uses of classical heritages within the educational and heritage sectors. It does so by exploring three significant and interrelated arenas where the heritages of classical antiquity are used to shape Danes as European citizens. Together, these three cases emphasise different but interconnected ways in which classical heritages are being put to use in order to construct Denmark's own distinctive national identity within Europe. Finally, the book also sheds light on some of the challenges that face unified and homogenous conceptions of European heritage and identity, as well as the notion of the "classical" itself.

Classical Heritage and European Identities is the first English-language monograph to situate the Danish case within the wider European context. As such, the book should be essential reading for researchers and students engaged in the study of heritage and museums, classics, education and modern European history.

Lærke Maria Andersen Funder is a Postdoctoral Research Fellow at the Department of History and Classical Studies, Aarhus University. Her research concentrates on the reception of antiquity, material culture and collections.

Troels Myrup Kristensen is Associate Professor of Classical Archaeology at Aarhus University and leads CoHERE's WP5. He works on ancient pilgrimage, visual culture and cultural heritage.

Vinnie Nørskov is Associate Professor of Classical Archaeology and Director of the Museum of Ancient Art and Archaeology at Aarhus University. Her research focuses on the uses of the classical past, the reception of classical antiquity, and the history of classical scholarship.

Critical Heritages of Europe
Series editors: Christopher Whitehead and Susannah Eckersley

The *Critical Heritages of Europe* series seeks to explore the cultural and social politics of the European past in the present. Bridging theoretical and empirical research, the series accommodates broad understandings of Europe – a shifting and historically mutable entity, made both of internal tensions and exogenous encounters, reimaginings and influences. "Heritage" also is taken as an expansive paradigm, made in myriad practices where the past is valorised for the present, from folk traditions to museums and memorials, the management of historic sites and traditions, and everyday matters such as education, political discourse, home life, food consumption and people's relations with place.

Books in the series engage with European heritages in *critical* times – in all senses – when Europe and mobilisations of its heritages and memories are called upon to solve problems and when contests over the meanings of the past are part of wider social and political relations and tensions. Heritage practices are variously informed by civil and uncivil visions, the politics of difference and copresence, difficult pasts, relations with the "outside," borders, margins and migrations. Critical questions include:

- What is the European past made to do in the present and for the future?
- What counts as European heritage? To whom, and why?
- How and why do relationships with, and attitudes to, the past inform identity positions, social orders and moral values in, or in relation to, Europe?
- When and where in the (wider) world do European heritages configure identities?
- What are the contemporary meanings and effects of global encounters, mobilities and trajectories in which Europe has played roles?
- What theoretical and critical perspectives can be articulated to contribute new understandings of European heritages? How might these be made relevant for current and future heritage practice?
- What are the relations between theory, criticality, ethics and heritage practice in the European dimension?

Selected titles:

Classical Heritage and European Identities
The Imagined Geographies of Danish Classicism
Lærke Maria Andersen Funder, Troels Myrup Kristensen and Vinnie Nørskov

For more information about this series, please visit: www.routledge.com/Critical-Heritages-of-Europe/book-series/COHERE

Classical Heritage and European Identities

The Imagined Geographies of Danish Classicism

Lærke Maria Andersen Funder, Troels Myrup Kristensen and Vinnie Nørskov

Routledge
Taylor & Francis Group

LONDON AND NEW YORK

First published 2019
by Routledge
2 Park Square, Milton Park, Abingdon, Oxon OX14 4RN

and by Routledge
52 Vanderbilt Avenue, New York, NY 10017

First issued in paperback 2020

Routledge is an imprint of the Taylor & Francis Group, an informa business

British Library Cataloguing-in-Publication Data
A catalogue record for this book is available from the British Library

Library of Congress Cataloging-in-Publication Data
A catalog record for this book has been requested

ISBN 13: 978-0-367-67026-9 (pbk)
ISBN 13: 978-1-138-31750-5 (hbk)

Typeset in Times New Roman
by Apex CoVantage, LLC

Contents

List of illustrations   vi
Preface   viii

1   Classical heritage and European identities:
    Introducing the Danish case   1

2   Classical antiquity in the Danish classroom:
    Oldtidskundskab as heritage   20

3   The imagined geographies of collecting: Displaying
    classical antiquity in Danish museums   45

4   Excavating a wonder of the ancient world: Danish
    classicism in the field   76

5   Becoming European: The critical heritage
    of Danish classicism   100

    Bibliography   106
    Index   123

Illustrations

Figures

1.1   Europe starts here! European Heritage Label at the entrance
      to the South Slope of the Athenian Acropolis, January 2018   2
1.2   Danish material claims to classical antiquity: The display of
      two marble heads, originally belonging to a metope from the
      Parthenon, on display in the National Museum in Copenhagen   9
1.3   Equestrian statue of Frederik V, Amalienborg, Copenhagen,
      by Jacques Saly (1754–1768)   12
2.1   Number of students with a degree from upper secondary
      school 1906–2017   22
3.1   Floor plan of the display of the National Museum's collection
      of classical antiquities   54
3.2   View of the National Museum's room 315, "The Roman World"   56
3.3   The "Copenhagen Vase," The National Museum. Attic
      red-figure vase, c. 500 BC. Bought for Prince Christian
      Frederik, the later King Christian VIII, in Paris 1839
      by archaeologist and naval officer C. T. Falbe   60
3.4   The Glyptotek as memorial: The Mausoleum façade with
      a relief by Carl Aarsleff showing Carl and Ottilia Jacobsen
      in Graeco-Roman costumes opposing a relief showing
      the personifications of Denmark and Copenhagen   63
3.5   The central hall with porticos and temple front with
      a memorial inscription for Carl and Ottilia   64
3.6   Map of the Ny Carlsberg Glyptotek from 2014 with plans
      of the displays of the collection of ancient sculpture and
      of "The Ancient Mediterranean"   65
3.7   Ny Carlsberg Glyptotek, room 8, Roman statue of Hercules   69
3.8   Ny Carlsberg Glypotek: Collection of sculpture in room 12,
      displaying the portraits from the Tomb of the Licinii.

The star piece, the portrait of Pompey the Great, is placed
at the centre of the arrangement   70
3.9 Ny Carlsberg Glyptotek, "The Ancient Mediterranean,"
room 25, under the thematic headline "The Many Faces
of the Romans," portraits illustrate the multicultural empire   72
4.1 Postcard from the 1909 National Exhibition (*Landsudstillingen*)
in Aarhus, showing classically inspired architecture, including a
Mausoleum-like pyramidal roof   77
4.2 The geography of Danish archaeological fieldwork in the
Mediterranean   82
4.3 Jeppesen's 1958 reconstruction of the Mausoleum   86
4.4 Jeppesen's Mausoleum reconstruction in the Museum
of Ancient Art and Archaeology, Aarhus   91
4.5 Jeppesen's Mausoleum reconstruction in Mausoleum
Museum, Bodrum   92
5.1 The classical past in the exhibition "Europe Meets the World"
at the National Museum in Copenhagen 2012. Socrates faces
Alexander the Great   101

Tables

2.1 Translations of tragedies by Aeschylus, Sophocles and
Euripides into Danish   31
4.1 Overview of Danish archaeological projects in Bodrum   97

Preface

The writing of this book was funded by the European Union's Horizon 2020 research and innovation programme under grant agreement no. 693289, awarded to "Critical Heritages (CoHERE): Performing and representing identities in Europe" and coordinated by Chris Whitehead, Newcastle University. We are grateful to Chris, Susannah Eckersley and all of our other CoHERE colleagues for creating such a stimulating and interdisciplinary environment for our research.

For her contribution to this book, Lærke Maria Anderson Funder received support from the Carlsberg Foundation, as part of her postdoctoral work within the collaborative research project "Cultural Encounter as a Precondition for European identities," directed by Marianne Pade, Danish Academy in Rome.

Portions of chapter 1 were previously published as part of Nørskov and Kristensen forthcoming. Chapter 3 is based partly on work carried out from Lærke Maria Andersen Funder's dissertation (Funder 2014) but has been updated and revised for this volume.

For assistance with our research, we are much indebted to Niels Bargfeldt, Gönül Bozoğlu, Poul Pedersen, and Birte Poulsen. We would also like to thank Isabelle Torrance for reading a draft of our manuscript. Lastly, we would like to thank Lucy Seton-Watson for linguistic revision of our manuscript, as well as Heidi Lowther for editorial guidance.

All translations from Danish and German are by the authors.

LMAF/TMK/VN
Aarhus, June 2018

1 Classical heritage and European identities

Introducing the Danish case

A large sign, carrying the blue and yellow insignia of the European Union (EU), greets visitors to the Athenian Acropolis, announcing in capital letters in Greek and English that "Europe starts here!" (Figure 1.1). The accompanying text spells out the long-term significance of the site for European identity (in the singular): "The Acropolis and its surrounding Archaeological Sites, the heart of Ancient Athens, is the place where the most essential aspects of the European identity emerged: Democracy, Philosophy, Theatre, Sciences, Arts."[1] The sign is a material manifestation of the fact that ancient Athens as a whole is the recipient of the European Heritage Label, instituted by the EU in 2013 and given to sites that are identified as having an intrinsic, symbolic value to European history.

The Acropolis sign, the heritage label that it represents, as well as the evocation of similar themes in the House of European History in Brussels are potent reminders of the continuous investment in classical (Greek and Roman) antiquity as a seemingly positive and harmonious foundation story in European history, in contrast to the dark and antagonistic heritage attributed to, for example, the Second World War or the Cold War. Official visits to Athens by Emmanuel Macron and Barack Obama in 2016 and 2017 respectively further demonstrate the level of this symbolic and political investment in Greece as the place where European and, by seemingly straightforward extension, Western civilisation began – a story that is also perpetuated in academic work (for example Meier 2011). In their public speeches in Athens, both the French and the US presidents construed Greece as the birthplace of Western democracy. Macron even linked the glory of Greece's past with the future of Europe – a statement that carried both symbolic potency and urgency when seen in light of the many political crises that currently face the continent.[2]

The European (and, more broadly, Western) use of classical antiquity as a role model that is evident in both the Acropolis sign and the presidents'

Figure 1.1 Europe starts here! European Heritage Label at the entrance to the South
Slope of the Athenian Acropolis, January 2018

Source: Photo courtesy of Troels Myrup Kristensen

Athenian speeches has origins going back to the Renaissance, when Italian
humanists turned the rediscovery of ancient texts into a new culture and
aesthetics (Baker 2015). Classicism, defined as applying models from classical antiquity in a prescriptive sense, developed from the Renaissance and
especially over the course of the "long" nineteenth century from the French
Revolution to the First World War into one of the most influential discourses
through which notions of civilisation, nationhood, citizenship and identity
were mirrored, constructed and prescribed. (Marchand 1996; Fögen and

Warren 2016). In this period, European art, architecture, science, education and civic institutions consciously evoked the diverse heritages of Greek and Roman antiquity, developing a shared, symbolic language that connected the contemporary ambitions of individual nations and their institutions with the seemingly eternal glory and grandeur of the classical past (Silk *et al.* 2014; see Raabyemagle and Smidt 1998 for Danish examples). Models from classical antiquity – not least the ideology of Roman imperialism – became powerful instruments in the administration of European colonies around the world, legitimising practices such as slavery and racism (Goff 2005; Bradley 2010). During the first part of the twentieth century, the appropriation of classical antiquity for political means experienced yet another dark chapter, when the Fascists in Italy and the Nazis in Germany actively used classicising models in their propaganda (Nelis 2008; Arthurs 2012). Today, contemporary uses of classical antiquity range from the highly nationalist and racist agendas of right-wing parties such as Greece's Golden Dawn (Hamilakis 2016) to the universalising and positive image of the "birthplace of Europe" as evoked by Macron, as well as the award of the European Heritage Label to the monuments of ancient Athens at large.

This book examines how different agents and institutions within the Danish nation state have situated themselves within this complex landscape of competing appropriations of classical antiquity from the eighteenth century to the present day. In particular, it focuses on the use of classical heritages to construct both European and national identities (in the plural) and especially on how Danes in this period have engaged with a sense of European commonality through their engagements with the classical past. Although Denmark was never geographically part of the ancient Greek or Roman world, it has a long tradition of employing classicism to provide models for contemporary society, citizenship culture and science. A precursor of this tradition goes back to the *Edda* of the thirteenth century, when the Icelandic poet and historian Snorri Sturluson (1179–1241) let the Norse gods be descendants of the Trojan kings (Stavnem 2011). Classicism intensified during the Renaissance and became firmly embedded in Danish national institutions from the late eighteenth century onwards. Its continued vitality is contingent on the dynamic adaptation of classical heritages, material as well as immaterial, into Danish cultural identities.

Like other Northern European countries situated beyond the Roman *limes* and even further away from the pinnacles of Mount Olympus, Denmark developed both a narrative and a *habitus* that linked itself with classical antiquity, not through some sense of spatial continuity but through its incorporation into an idea of a common European heritage in which Denmark was believed to have an important share. Even if this discourse is centuries old and has never been hegemonic, it continues to shape important aspects of how the

Danish nation defines itself. For instance, as we were writing this book, Mette Bock, the current Danish Minister of Culture and Member of Parliament for the Liberal Alliance, declared in an interview with a major newspaper that Danes would benefit from reading more Plato (Kassebeer 2017).

Through its location between continental Europe and the other Nordic countries, Denmark can be seen as a liminal or transitional area that often finds itself split between European and Nordic identities, something that has been evident in Danish politics in the past 50 years, not least in the country's ambiguous relationship with the EU (Miles and Wivel 2014; Hansen 2001, 2002). Denmark joined the EU (then the European Economic Community) in 1973, but on several occasions the country has rejected closer integration during referendums on the Maastricht Treaty in 1992, the European Monetary Union in 2000 and the so-called opt-outs in 2015. Furthermore, Denmark's classical heritage (and by implication, its identity as a European country) has historically competed with Nordic or even entirely national notions of identity, often in complex ways.[3] For example, the right-wing nationalist and EU-sceptic Danish People's Party (*Dansk Folkeparti*) has on several occasions defended the place of the classics in Danish education by referring to their role in introducing students more broadly to history and culture, in spite of their otherwise rigid emphasis on what is perceived as specifically Danish heritage, such as the Viking monuments at Jelling (Niklasson and Hølleland 2018).

The central argument of this book is that the continual employment and appropriation of classical heritages in the Danish context constitutes a significant case of an imagined geography, which places the birth of European identity within the culture-historical imaginary of classical antiquity. Through three case studies, we intend to demonstrate how this imagined geography has been embedded and even naturalised in distinctive ways within the educational and heritage sectors. The case studies explore three significant and interrelated arenas in which classical heritages are used to construct particular identities and to shape Danes as European citizens. In the following sections, we lay out the book's theoretical framework, especially the intersection between classical reception studies and the emerging field of critical heritage studies, as well as the concept of imagined geography and how it is applied in our analysis of the relationship between identity, nationalism and classicism in Denmark. Finally, we turn to the empirical and methodological background for the three case studies.

Classicism as critical heritage

The book implements a critical historiographical perspective in line with recent work in classical reception that has stressed the dialectical relationship between past, present and future (Settis 2006; Martindale 2006;

Hardwick and Stray 2008; Prettejohn 2012; Hanink 2017). It thus contributes to a large and growing body of scholarship at the intersection between Classical Studies (in which the study of postantique appropriations of classical antiquity has become increasingly common) and Heritage Studies (which among other things has explored more generally how people use the past to construct particular identities to shape present and future: Smith 2006; Harrison 2013; Macdonald 2013). This section provides a brief overview of some of the key developments in these fields in order to contextualise the book's arguments within their broader theoretical setting.

The study of postantique uses of classical heritage is often carried out under the umbrella of classical reception, implying a passive process of transmission from classical antiquity to more recent periods. There is indeed a long tradition of undertaking studies on the rediscovery of classical antiquity by artists and architects, including in Danish scholarship, where, for example, the grand tour travels of Danish painters and sculptors have been traced in great detail (prominent examples include Nielsen 1990; Bendtsen 1993; Dietz 1999; Christiansen 2000; Fejfer *et al.* 2003; Nørskov 2008; Nielsen and Rathje 2010). Traditional studies have also investigated collecting practices and the formation of museum collections that forged a material link to the classical past that was not recoverable from the Danish soil (for instance, Krogh and Guldager Bilde 1997; Nørskov 2002; Rasmussen *et al.* 2000; Moltesen 2012). In the most recent wave of classical reception studies (Martindale 2007, 2013; Hardwick 2003), the scope of the discipline in terms of its material and approach has been substantially broadened. Charles Martindale has highlighted how reception denotes a dynamic and reciprocal process of understanding that "illuminates antiquity as much as modernity" (Martindale 2013, 171). Classical antiquity constantly mutates as we engage with it from our own historical and contextual place in time. In the continually developing process of reception, new and unexplored aspects of antiquity come into focus through the changing contexts of interpretation (Martindale 2013, 181). This more nuanced, critical approach to reception studies is increasingly incorporated into the study of classics. It has transformed the discipline from a positivistic and normative tradition that essentially confirms classical antiquity as a "world that had nurtured civilisations and whose achievements eclipsed anything accomplished by Western Europe until the Renaissance" (Vasunia and Stephens 2010, 3) towards a reflective, poststructural and hermeneutically informed practice that is conscious of its own temporal and cultural situatedness and influence.

Embedded in the above understanding of the reception and use of classical heritage is a notion of time as cyclical. In Salvatore Settis's thoughtful and in-depth discussion of the complexity of the "classical" as concept and phenomenon (2006), he presents its many meanings and uses as well as underlining cultural preconditions. The concept of classicism as we understand it as synonymous with Greek and Roman culture was not established before the early nineteenth century, but it builds on a conceptualisation of memory and the past that is based on a dichotomy between ancient and modern that developed in the early Renaissance (Settis 2006, 56–99). The idea of rebirth that underpins the idea of classicism – expressed literally in the use of the term *Renaissance* to denote a historical period – implies death and then recovery, building on an organic idea of life as a model of historical thinking with a rhythmical process of deaths and rebirths. The word *classical* also implies ideas about values and ideals defining, on the one hand, "first class" and, on the other, a specific aesthetic that is harmonious, balanced and moderate (Settis 2006, 64–65). In this is implied an elitist, Western set of values that has in recent years been questioned. In reception studies, this has been defined as a "democratic turn," drawing inspiration from postcolonial and feminist theory. The democratic turn entails three perspectives that have been fundamental to current reception studies (Hardwick and Stray 2008, 3). Firstly, it questions the notion of the inherent superiority and normative power of classical culture in the West (Joshel *et al.* 2001; Cuno 2008; Bilsel 2012); secondly, it investigates and challenges the traditional conceptualisation of classics as belonging exclusively to the elite; and, thirdly, it turns the attention towards how classics has been received and appropriated in much wider social contexts, including outside Europe (Hall 2008; McElduff 2006; Paul 2010, 2013). In this book, we use this scholarship to nuance and contextualise the sometimes narrow and one-dimensional Danish discussions of the value of classical heritage.

We also draw on insights from the emerging field of critical heritage studies in order to provide a broader view of classical antiquity as heritage. Sharon Macdonald defines *heritage* as places that can be visited; and classical heritage sites are traditionally perceived as places around the Mediterranean, (Macdonald 2013, 23). However, through imagined geography, this concept can be extended to a cognitive and imaginative sphere, as will be discussed below. The concept of critical heritage underscores not only its material aspects but also a critical approach to the inherent *valuation* that is at the core of sustaining something as heritage (Macdonald 2013, 18). The act of valuating aspects of the past, imbuing them with certain qualities, discursively establishes them as heritage. While the term *heritage* inherently comprises a central material aspect, the discursive operations inherent in selecting, preserving and perpetuating certain aspects of the past imbue it with an intangible aspect as well, as it becomes a way of understanding the world (Macdonald 2013, 18; Smith 2006, 43). These discursive operations are often implemented in the context of cultural and political institutions such as museums, academia, and the educational sector. Once something is established as "heritage," it is open to a constant dialectic between cultural and political confirmation and contestation (Smith 2006, 82). This is due to the nature of heritage as always belonging to a specific location and group of people (Macdonald 2013; Smith 2006, 3). Heritage can "turn the past from something that is simply there, or has merely happened, into an arena from which selections can be made and values derived . . . turning the past into The Past" (Macdonald 2013, 18). In this view, heritage is a production of "The Past" in a given present (Harrison 2013, 32). Such normative views of an authorised heritage discourse have been very influential in the naturalisation of classical heritage in Denmark, as we will see in our case studies, and we will use scholarship from critical heritage studies to interpret the different ways in which different agents – both institutions and individuals – have shaped discourses of classicism in the Danish context.

Imagined geography

In order to grasp the role of classical heritage for identity building in an non-classical country, we have implemented the concept of imagined geography as an analytical tool. The concept provides a framework in which to read and interpret various uses and definitions of classical antiquity observed both in the Danish educational system and more broadly in the cultural heritage sector. We begin with a discussion of the concept of imagined geography, building on work by cultural studies scholar Edward Said and political scientist Benedict Anderson, and we discuss how it can be identified in particular key discourses that relate to classical heritage.

Imaginative geography – a close variant of the term – is used on several occasions in Said's highly influential *Orientalism* (Said 1978), although Said refrains from defining the concept explicitly. Said uses "imaginative geography" to refer to a particular way of ascribing meaning to geography on the basis of cultural tropes and in terms of binary oppositions, for example the loaded antithesis of East and West. Such tropes contain numerous layers of ideological baggage and constitute ways of naturalising a particular world view based on factoids (Said 1978, 71). Through imaginative geography, European scholars and artists have for centuries described the Near East as undeveloped and eternally Other. Orientalism is an exploration of what Said calls the "essential motifs of European imaginative geography" (Said 1978, 57). He traces such motifs in a range of different contexts that in effect constitute a highly toxic form of geographical determinism, which has important implications in the present. Said's work has been criticised for its focus on textual constructions of Orientalism, but it serves as a starting point for this discussion of the relationship between power and knowledge.

In *Imagined Communities*, Benedict Anderson's equally influential study of the origins of nationalism in the late eighteenth century, the nation is characterised as "an imagined political community" (Anderson 2016, 6; on its influence on Danish historiography, see Mentz 2004). Anderson continues: "It is imagined because the members of even the smallest nation will never know most of their fellow-members, meet them, or even hear of them, yet in the minds of each lives the image of their communion" (Anderson 2016, 6). The communities of the nation state are thus bound together through shared narratives, images and, indeed, myths. One particularly useful aspect of Anderson's work in this context is the power with which the act of "imagining" is imbued: It is seemingly able to justify colossal sacrifices, notably in the service of state-sponsored violence. Although Anderson did not write his work from a postmodernist perspective, a pertinent influence of his concept in later work has been the study of the nation as a set of discourses that can be deconstructed (Smith 1998, 142). Anderson has been rightly criticised for paying little attention to materialisations of the imagined community, for example, those monuments that tie the nation together. As we shall see especially in chapters 3 and 4, the material aspects of imagined geography are indeed fundamental.

Imagined geography, as used here, refers to the creative ability of a given nation – as well as subgroups and individuals within that nation – to construct geography-driven discourses of identity. This sense of imagined geography acknowledges that there are always omissions and interruptions in the way that history is written and the way that identity is forged. An imagined geography can be based on "here" – that is, a place-based imagining of identity – as in the case of the Athenian Acropolis, which is fundamental in representations of the modern Greek nation and which remains one of the country's most important "theatres of memory" (Yalouri 2001; Hamilakis 2007, 85–98). At the same time, through a whole range of imagined geographies constructed on European essentialising tropes such as the "West" and "the birthplace of democracy" (as we already observed in relation to Figure 1.1), the Acropolis is claimed as European or even world heritage, as recently exploited by Macron and Obama during their visits. This example thus shows how the imagined geographies of a place connect several different scales of heritage, from the local to the global. Imagined geography thus becomes particularly layered when it operates with a "there" by transferring claims of a particular place or memory to somewhere else, as in the case of the Bavarian Walhalla, which was built as a copy of the Parthenon in Athens (even if its name evokes Norse mythology) and served as a hall of memory for the first Bavarian, then German state and its heroes. In the same way, collections of classical antiquities may be understood as representative of this imagined geography. The case of the Parthenon marbles – which were moved from the Athenian Acropolis by

Lord Elgin to Britain, where they have been displayed in the British Museum in London since 1817 – is perhaps the best-known example of classical works claimed as world heritage, but every collection of classical antiquities partakes in this process of appropriation that reconfigures a particular country's place in the world. The prominent position in the Danish National Museum given to two small heads belonging to the Parthenon's metopes that were bought by Captain Moritz Hartmann in the streets of Athens in 1687 constitutes a powerful Danish example of how classical antiquities may participate in discourses of imagined geography within museum spaces (Figure 1.2).

Figure 1.2 Danish material claims to classical antiquity: The display of two marble heads, originally belonging to a metope from the Parthenon, on display in the National Museum in Copenhagen

Source: Photo courtesy of Lærke Maria Andersen Funder

Creating an imagined geography entails imbuing physical spaces with immaterial concepts: values, ideals and properties. These operations are what turn the Athenian Acropolis from a space to a place (Yalouri 2001). In characterising the effects of these operations, philosopher Jeff Malpas distinguishes between the concepts of space and place, stating that while space "tends towards the homogenous, the regular, and the uniform," place "is defined by relation to the notion of bound, limit or surface" and is "a locus of meaning, memory and identity" (Malpas 2014, 4; see also Malpas 2012; Berry 2009). The concept of place is defined both by its relation to other places and through the creation of new relations and new places that add temporality through those processes. This conceptualisation of place incorporates a diachronic and contextual idea of identity formation, showing how the human experience is played out within and across networks of places (Malpas 2014, 4, 11–12). The process of turning space into place is essentially discursive, but in the extended sense of the term, it involves material as well as immaterial elements. An archaeological excavation with its description, documentation and interpretation can be seen as a process of "place-making." Likewise, a museum exhibition transforms from a space to a place through the collection and organisation of the objects and information on display, very often referring to other places – and indeed helping to define these places further. School curricula are another example of textual and visual discourses in which place may be constituted through historical and cultural qualifications of geographical areas, which in turn are made meaningful in relation to the students' own cultural context. In this way the concept of imagined geography is applied as a perspective through which identity as connected to culture, heritage and place can be explored. In the following chapters we thus argue that the Danish discourse of classicism can be defined as an imagined geography through a series of cultural practices and constructed narratives that extend beyond the borders of the nation state and that construct a particular notion of European identity.

Danish nationhood and European identities

Current academic research into the nexus between culture, identity and heritage in a European context operates with a consensus that all three concepts must be understood in the plural – in contrast to the singular construction of European identity as construed on the sign at the entrance to the Acropolis (Delanty 2013; Macdonald 2013; Whitehead *et al.* 2015). The plurality of identities, cultures and heritages is a challenge especially to academic subjects with a normative, paradigmatic history that is embedded in large societal institutions such as curricula, museums or field practices such as archaeological excavations. It is also a challenge to a nation such as

Denmark, which is one of the oldest monarchies in Europe. Historian Uffe Østergaard has defined the Danish nation state as "a rare situation of virtual identity between state, nation and society" (Østergaard 1992, 3), seemingly leaving little room for plurality. This is, however, a more recent phenomenon than is normally recognised in Denmark: "It is very hard to question what seems natural. This certainly applies to the sense of belonging to a nation, so totally taken for granted in modern times – particularly by the Danes" (Hall, Korsgaard and Pedersen 2015, 3). Danish nation-building and identity construction are traditionally situated in a local political, economic and social crisis of the nineteenth century. In this section, this process is discussed with a special focus on the meaning and role of classicism in the development of national identities, specifically focusing on the case of Denmark, while also pointing to key developments in other European countries.

Going back to the Renaissance, classical antiquity had been established as a paradigmatic part of European culture, constituting a cross-national dimension of classicism that could be defined as universal from this point onwards. In the centuries following the birth of humanism in fourteenth-century Italy, the power of the classical past as an ideal and as a source for construction of regional and local cultural identities was honed across Europe (Weiss 1969; Barkan 1999; Díaz-Andreu 2001, 430). Consequently, the cultural elites established classical heritage as valuable cultural capital in Europe before the establishment of the modern nation state. Europe's cultural and economic elite looked first to classical antiquity, but during the sixteenth century they increasingly appropriated their own local pasts for the construction of a historical foundation for their nations. The past in all its forms – literature, art and architecture – was recorded, collected, imitated and appropriated in order to take possession of its paradigmatic power of making identities (Miller 2017). Thereby, a dual dimension of local versus universal pasts was embedded into the reception and appropriation of the past.

Despite the competition from local pasts in Scandinavia, formulated through Gothicism (Norris 2016; Rix 2011), classical antiquity became central in imagining a European ideal in Renaissance Denmark. An important part of the early studies of Gothicism was in fact to trace connections between classical and Swedish history, establishing the Goths as the culture from which the Greeks originated (Siapkas 2017, 62–63). This link was as mentioned, established already in the Icelandic *Edda*. Through Christianity, Latin arrived in Denmark with the Catholic Church, and among the learned clerks the interest in classical texts grew (Horster and Funder 2017). After the Reformation, the Danish elites participated in the European patterns of building up royal collections, founding universities and, later, art academies. With the establishment of absolute monarchy in 1660 over a composite state consisting of the kingdoms of Denmark and Norway, the duchies of

Schleswig and Holstein, the North Atlantic territories of Greenland, Iceland and the Faroe Islands, and adding colonies in the West Indies, West Africa and India, the Danish monarchy belonged to one of the largest European multinational states (Østergaard 1992, 3, 2004, 25–29). Classicism during this period, up to around 1800, was embedded in aristocratic and royal symbolic language that appropriated especially the Roman imperial language of power through royal architectural settings such as Frederiksborg Castle (1602–1625) and equestrian statues of Danish kings (Figure 1.3).

During the eighteenth century, the Enlightenment and a process of institutionalisation had placed classical heritage in a central position in the Danish cultural landscape. Through the application of a classical formal language in education and in art and architecture, an imagined geography was established that connected Denmark to a broader European community of nobilities and intellectuals. Denmark partook in both the formulation and the diffusion of classicism on a European scale, whereby individuals and their European connections played a key role in integrating core ideas of classicism both in Denmark and in Europe (Kryger 1991). The Danish

Figure 1.3 Equestrian statue of Frederik V, Amalienborg, Copenhagen, by Jacques Saly (1754–1768)

Source: Photo courtesy of Troels Myrup Kristensen

sculptor Johannes Wiedewelt (1731–1802) was a close friend of the influential art historian Johann Joachim Winckelmann (1717–1768) and translated his work into Danish (Nielsen and Rathje 2010). Wiedewelt was instrumental in the foundation of the Royal Art Academy in Copenhagen in 1754. Neoclassicism became very strong in Denmark, not least through the work of the sculptor Bertel Thorvaldsen (1770–1844), who lived and worked for most of his life in Rome. Thorvaldsen's collection and works were donated to the Danish state and became the first public museum in Denmark when it opened in 1848 (Melander 1993). Heirs to this tradition, the two Danish architects Christian (1803–1883) and Theophilius Hansen (1813–1891) were among the prime European agents in developing neoclassicism as a common European architectural language in Athens, Vienna and Copenhagen (Jørgensen and Porphyrios 1987; Panourgiá 2004). The Hansen brothers illustrate well how the international networks of the elite were essential in the diffusion of classicism as a strong symbolic language of an imagined geography across Europe.

Margarita Díaz-Andreu has identified neoclassicism as the root of the civic nationalism that defined Europe up until the 1870s (Díaz-Andreu 2001, 431). In civic nationalism, the key concepts were citizenship, territory and equal rights for all citizens based on civilisation through universal education in classical cultures. Civilisation is here opposed to ethnic nationalism, which focused on the local national culture (Jørgensen 2005, 97–98; Daugbjerg 2011, 11). The civic nationalism developing in Denmark was patriotic, true to the King, and rooted in a small nobility and an elite educational system. Claus Møller Jørgensen divides the classical heritage of European civilisation into a Latin/French aesthetic tradition and a neohumanistic Greek/German tradition (Jørgensen 2005). The aesthetic tradition was strong in the visual arts, as seen above, whereas the neohumanistic tradition became essential in the educational system.

The broader European conception of civilisation as building on classical heritage was completely embedded in Danish education and culture by the turn of the eighteenth century. Classical education was considered essential, and the Greek and Latin languages were the most important subjects in school. Even the teaching of Danish was carried out on the basis of classical literature, as Danish literature was considered less sophisticated than the classical and authors could only proceed to a higher standard if they were learning style and rhetoric from Greek and Roman writers (Jørgensen 2005, 105). As in other European countries, learning and education were in the hands of the Church and were mainly limited to the literate classes until the late eighteenth century (cf. Adams 2015 on England). Public schools first became widespread in Europe from the late eighteenth century, and in Denmark compulsory learning was implemented with the first school law covering all children in 1814. This came simultaneously with a widespread recognition of local languages. Danish became a school subject in 1775, and language emerged as a key element in the definition of Danish identity during the nineteenth century.

For the Danish development, the connection to Germany was absolutely paramount. As Suzanne Marchand has pointed out, philhellenism in Germany was a process of aligning the ideals from ancient Greece with aristocratic models and, during the nineteenth century, institutionalising them in research institutions, schools and museums – all essential educational institutions (Marchand 1996, xvii–xix). Danish educational systems were modelled on the German during this period of institutionalisation, and a key concept in this development was *Bildung*, translated in Danish into *dannelse*. This concept still plays a fundamental role in discourses on education in Denmark, now using the extended form of *Allgemeinbildung* (*almendannelse* in Danish). Many authors struggle to translate these concepts into English. In this book we have chosen to keep the German *Bildung* and translate *Allgemeinbildung* into general education.

The political and social changes of the late eighteenth and early nineteenth centuries in Europe affected profoundly the stable and prospering Danish monarchy. In order to benefit economically, Denmark tried to remain neutral in the conflict between France and the rest of Europe after the French revolution. However, Denmark eventually used its military to secure free trade and thus provoked an attack from Great Britain in 1801 and 1807, resulting in the loss of the navy, a state bankruptcy in 1813, and the loss of Norway in 1814 (Hansen 2001, 115–119; Østergaard 2004, 29; Daugbjerg 2011, 11). In postrevolutionary Europe, the diminished Danish state turned to a Danish or Nordic past to define and develop an imagined national community. The systematic collection of archaeological artefacts from Danish soil began with the foundation of the Antiquities Commission in 1807 (Jensen 1992). Classical antiquities were also collected from this time onwards, as will be discussed in chapter 3. It is worth emphasising that these local and classical collections were not exclusive, but existed in the royal collections side by side. It is through disciplinary developments during the nineteenth century that archaeologies came to be defined as different. This was as much a political as a scientific process (Whitehead 2009).

The turn towards ethnic nationalism, with a stronger focus on the local past, accelerated in the 1830s and 1840s, implying a strong romantic and organic relationship between antiquities, nationalism and identity (Daugbjerg 2011, 11–12). It was expressed by the Danish archaeologist and later director of the National Museum Jens Jacob Asmussen Worsaae in 1840/41 when he defined the power of the past to "awaken the sensibility for our magnificent antiquities and the deference of the fatherland and the honour of our nationality that is inseparable from them" (cited from Daugbjerg 2011, 12). In this sense, heritage has been instrumental in defining Danish identity since the early nineteenth century. As has been pointed out, Denmark was the first European country to draw on excavations and exhibitions of national antiquities as part of the project of constructing a national identity, as opposed to classical and Near Eastern antiquities (Díaz-Andreu 2001, 432–434; Daugbjerg 2011, 11). This may be one of the reasons why classicism has received very little attention in studies of nationalism and identity in nineteenth-century Denmark (Bang 2005). Indeed, a wide-ranging study on identity published in 1991–1992 contains practically no mention of classical heritage in nineteenth-century development (Feldbæk 1991–1992).

A significant aspect of the development of Danish nationalism during the nineteenth century is the role of the peasants. Uffe Østergaard has demonstrated how they during the nineteenth century developed into a strong political entity in Denmark. A growing non-elite nationalism among the farmers was one of the foundations for the movement of the priest, author, philosopher and poet Nikolaj Frederik Severin Grundtvig (1783–1872), whose concepts of the people and the national as culturally defined were heavily inspired by Herder's ideas about the relationship between people, nation and culture (Daugbjerg 2011; Larsen and Larsen 2011, 251–254). Grundtvig was an essential figure in the reform of the Church – not only through his revivalist thinking and the more than 1,500 psalms that are one of his most prolific legacies, but also through the educational system (Østergaard 1992, 6–11; Rerup 1993; Haue 2003, 52–53; Hall, Korsgaard and Petersen 2015). Through the *Folkehøjskole* (Folk High School), an independent educational institution that was essential in providing an education for ordinary people, Grundtvig democratised education. The schools were key elements in the growing self-esteem of Danish farmers, who came to constitute an alternative elite (Østergaard 1992, 13–14).

The political engagement of the peasants was at first local and regional, but in the 1870s they joined in the united "Left" party (*Det Forenede Venstre*). By then, the Danish state had been completely transformed: first through the peaceful revolution of 1848/49, leading to the change to a constitutional regime with a democratically elected parliament, and second through a bloody war with Prussia over the two German duchies, in which Denmark's defeat in 1864 reduced the country to a very small and humiliated state. With the defeat, Danish nationalism was boosted through the famous saying "Outward losses must be made up by inward gains" (cited from Østergaard 2004, 32). In this new environment, the peasants were not the only constituency to promote a strong national sentiment. A new class of industrial entrepreneurs took over the values and cultural symbols of the declining old nobility. One essential figure was J. C. Jacobsen (1811–1887), who founded the Carlsberg breweries. He was active in politics, and he invested in national culture through the total rebuilding of the burnt-out Frederiksborg Castle, which was transformed into a Museum of National History. His most influential activity, however, was the establishment of the Carlsberg Foundation as proprietor of the breweries. Jacobsen secured the connection to science by donating the foundation to the Royal Danish Academy of Sciences and Letters in 1876 (Glamann 1976). It has since then supported academic research, not least within classical archaeology. Beginning with the excavation of Lindos, the Carlsberg Foundation has been fundamental to Danish archaeological projects in the Mediterranean. Unlike the German excavations, which were sponsored by the government, the Danish projects demonstrate a particularly close relationship between public and private donors in Danish archaeology. The Carlsberg Foundation's investment in the Rhodes excavation, together with earlier expeditions to Greenland and the construction of the Ny Carlsberg Glyptotek, were part of the larger nation-building remit of the Carlsberg Foundation. Crudely stated, the mission of the foundation – which has continued to have close ties with Danish academia – amounts to what could be called a public-private partnership with the overarching aim of modernising Denmark and making proper cultured Europeans of its citizens (cf. chapter 2).

Marchand identifies art and archaeology as essential materials in the process of Hellenisation in Germany; in fact, she argues that what made Greek culture the choice among others when Germany was searching for past cultures as sources of renewal was the materialisation of the aesthetic in large marble sculptures (Marchand 1996, xix, 5). Collections of ancient art constituted an essential part of the cultural expression of identity building in the rising nation states in Europe. The British Museum in London and the Louvre in Paris were material manifestations of imperial ambition, and through the layout of their collections, classical art was constructed in a chronological framework as the birth of European culture. Marble sculpture had not been very dominant in the Danish royal collections, which had focused on Greek painted pottery. This changed following the collecting activities of J. C. Jacobsen's son, Carl Jacobsen (1842–1914) who amassed one of the largest sculpture collections in Northern Europe in the late nineteenth century founding the Ny Carlsberg Glyptotek, thereby placing Denmark, a small country, in the same league as the large European states through its classical collections (cf. chapter 3).

Three case studies

The following chapters develop the lines of enquiry in three different arenas: education, collecting and archaeological fieldwork. Chapter 2 focuses on the subject entitled Classical Studies (in Danish *Oldtidskundskab*), which has been compulsory in Danish upper secondary schools (*gymnasieskolen*) since 1903 and which remains one of the most important settings through which Danes encounter classical heritage. In the nineteenth century, the educational system experienced increased pressure from outside to widen the subjects taught by the addition of natural science and mathematics. This development forced politicians to consider the role of individual subjects in teaching either as part of the general education in the tradition of *Bildung* or as concrete skills to the productive benefit of society. In this crossfire, classical languages became a contested area. The chapter analyses the development of the educational system in the nineteenth century that led to the invention of this new subject, named after the German *Altertumswissenschaft*. When we focus on the discourses preceding the invention of Classical Studies and those appearing during the twentieth century, when the subject was threatened with closure, it becomes clear that the cultural heritage particularly of ancient Greek culture was perceived as essential in understanding Danish culture in a European context. In this respect, the subject creates an imagined geography linking Denmark to Europe, which is particularly influential given its wide reach to all students in upper secondary school.

In chapter 3, we turn to the public museum. The role of the museum as a site for the education of the people has been present since the inception of public museums in Denmark, when Christian Jürgensen Thomsen gave private tours around the Nordic Museum, which became the National Museum of Denmark in 1892. The classical collection in the National Museum was originally part of the royal collection and was expanded by Christian VIII. The chapter presents an analysis of the exhibitions of the National Museum and the Ny Carlsberg Glyptotek at the turn of the twenty-first century. It demonstrates how the representations of classical antiquity in the permanent displays are rendered as Danish national and international cultural identities, and how these displays situate Denmark in a European cultural landscape. The chapter focuses on the permanent displays because the exhibition format is grounded in objects from the permanent collection and thus represents a historicity of interpretation of this body of objects within a given institution. While the displays express the preferences of the institution at the given time and context within which the displays were created (Gade 2006, 22), they also reflect the ethos and traditions of the institution. Therefore, the history of the classical collections, and how they entwine not only classicism but also the museum institution in a Danish conceptualisation of belonging to a European culture, will figure as a background against which the current displays can be understood.

Whereas the preceding two chapters focus on discourses of classicism within the borders of the nation state of Denmark itself, chapter 4 turns to Bodrum (ancient Halikarnassos, now located in modern Turkey) as one of the most important sites abroad where Danish archaeologists have been active in recovering classical heritage from the ground for more than 50 years. The importance of Bodrum in broader discourses of classicism is twofold. Firstly, the city is the birthplace of the Greek historian Herodotus (c. 480–c. 425 BC), who takes a central place in the curriculum of *Old-tidskundskab*. Secondly, it is home to the Mausoleum, which was built in 353–330 BC for the burial of Maussollos, the Persian satrap of Karia, and his sister-wife Artemisia II and considered to be one of the seven wonders of the ancient world. Danish fieldwork in Bodrum began formally in 1966 with Kristian Jeppesen's excavations at the site of the Mausoleum. Later Danish work has expanded to focus on other parts of the city and its surrounding archaeological landscapes. In 2016, the Danish fieldwork in Bodrum celebrated its 50th anniversary, which makes it the longest-ever Danish archaeological project in the Mediterranean. Students and professors from all three Danish universities that offer teaching in classical archaeology have participated in this fieldwork. Bodrum is thus a significant site of Danish classical heritage production, and one which, in turn, plays an important role in a variety of identity constructions. In light of Bodrum's location in modern Turkey, which has a long and complex relationship with Europe in its own right, this is a place where the Danish imagined geography of classical heritage is continuously confronted with the geopolitics of the present.

Together, these three case studies emphasise different but interconnected ways in which classical heritages are being put to use in order to construct Denmark's imagined geography and its own distinctive national identity within Europe. They show how Danish public and private investment in classical antiquity builds on a desire to connect with an ideal of the European nation state that can be traced back to the eighteenth century, if not earlier. classical heritages have thus historically been central components in the national imagination in Denmark. Partly for this reason, they have also been contested, and they continue to be challenged in new ways in the present by political, economic and cultural shifts.

Notes

1 Original capitalisation. Athens was awarded the European Heritage Label in 2014 based on a report by experts (https://ec.europa.eu/programmes/creative-europe/actions/heritage-label_en). The report explains Athens' European significance in more detail: "The heart of Ancient Athens comprises nearly 100 monuments of European significance, such as the Acropolis hill, the Pnyx hill, and the Kerameikos cemetery. They make up a rich historical landscape where events fundamental to the formation of essential aspects of European culture and identity took place, from the development of classical art and theatre, to democracy, equal rights, and science. These monuments witnessed the birth and upbringing of key figures in European history whose intellectual achievements made an indelible mark on the definition of European common values as expressed in a variety of areas ranging from political and legal thought (Pericles), art and architecture (Phidias),

literature and drama (Aeschylus, Sophocles, Euripides), medicine and science (Hippocrates), historical writing and the construction [of] memory (Herodotus, Thucydides), just to name a few." Athens also served as the first European Capital of Culture in 1985. Currently no Danish site has been awarded the European Heritage Label.

2 Text and video of Macron's speech at the Pnyx on 7 September 2017 are available online: www.elysee.fr/declarations/article/discours-du-president-de-la-republique-emmanuel-macron-a-la-pnyx-athenes-le-jeudi-7-septembre-201/ (last visited 3 May 2018).

3 A case in point is www.Danmarkshistorien.dk, a widely used web resource on Danish history that does not include any discussion of classical heritage.

2   Classical antiquity in the Danish classroom

Oldtidskundskab as heritage

The educational system is the essential communicator of cultural heritage. Inevitably, therefore, it is a battlefield of political, social and ideological discourses on the role and content of education for society (Jensen 2008, 45). The point of departure in this chapter is the invention in 1903 of a new mandatory subject in Danish secondary school (*gymnasium*), Classical Studies (in Danish, *Oldtidskundskab*).

Seen in a European perspective, Classical Studies was a new approach in general education and has become a Danish speciality. Discussions about how much Greek and Latin should be taught compared to other subjects took place in most European countries as natural sciences and modern languages came to be seen as more and more relevant for society at large. In Classical Studies, students were to learn about Greek culture, not by learning the language but by reading texts in translation and by studying classical art and architecture. Rather than a study of language, therefore, Classical Studies became primarily a study of literature. The most recent study plan for Classical Studies, defines the subject as dealing with the knowledge and culture of classical antiquity as the basis of European and global culture:

> Classical Studies is a subject that deals with knowledge, information and culture from classical antiquity as the foundation of the art and imagination of later periods in Europe as well as globally. The subject is central in the general education of the students because it deals with ancient texts and monuments expressing values, concepts and idioms that became normative in later periods' art, literature, thinking and values.
>
> (Stx-læreplaner 2017)

This definition is the product of negotiations concerning the role and legitimacy of Classical Studies in Denmark that have been in progress for more than 100 years. In spite of its name, the subject originally focused exclusively on Greek culture because it was a substitute for learning ancient Greek. Since its inception, the chronological and cultural framework of Classical Studies has broadened. Likewise, the number of students being taught Classical Studies has increased enormously in this period as the general level of education has risen. In 1906 462 students finished the gymnasium (403 males and 59 females); in 1975 12,564 finished (for the first time there were more female than male students); and in 2017 26,910 finished with the mandatory subject of Classical Studies (Figure 2.1). In 2017 the number was equivalent to 37 percent of the year group, more than one-third of all young Danes (Fakta 2015, 3).[1] Thus a much larger cohort of Danish society today has knowledge of Greek culture than when the subject was invented in 1903 when the percentage was about one. In this respect the introduction of the subject paved the way for classical antiquity to become transformed, with the spread of mass education in the twentieth century, from being elitist knowledge restricted to the few to becoming appropriated, first by the growing bourgeoisie and eventually by the general public. But for Classical Studies, knowledge of Greek and Roman culture in Danish society would have been a highly specialised niche – as it is for Egyptology and Assyriology, for instance.

This chapter will explore the negotiations and their consequences for the conceptualisation of Classical Studies. The social and political discussions will be analysed in order to define the role of the classical past in the Danish educational system but also to explore how classical antiquity has been conceptualised and performed in the classroom. Which classical past was deemed relevant in a Danish context, and why? In order to answer these questions, what could be called an excavation of the historical arguments and counterargument will be carried out. Firstly, the preconditions for and invention of the subject will be discussed, specifically how the connection with Europe was constructed in an imagined geography and which heritages are at play in the linkage drawn between Denmark and classical antiquity during the nineteenth century. Since its invention, the legitimacy of the subject in the Danish school system has been challenged several times. The question of legitimacy is defined here as a challenge, and when a system is challenged it generates anxiety, insecurity and the need to argue for preservation of the status quo. At this point, arguments become noticeably more clearly expressed. Thus, secondly, these "challenges" will be explored, with the aim of defining the tropes that have been developed and established in the discourse on the legitimation of the subject.

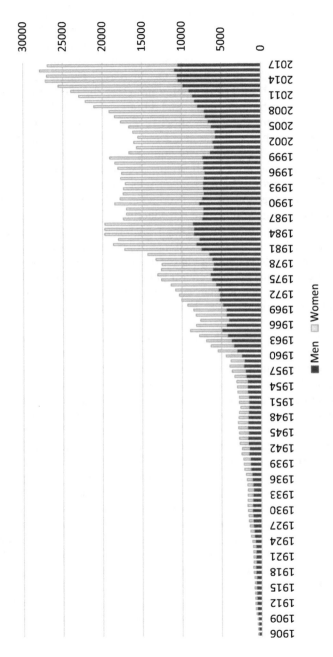

Figure 2.1 Number of students with a degree from upper secondary school 1906–2017

Greek and Latin

In the middle of the nineteenth century, the progression to university studies went through the so-called learned schools (*lærde skoler*) that replaced the Latin schools during the reform process of 1805–1809, as teaching became transformed by the neohumanism that spread especially from Germany. Latin was still the main subject, followed by Greek, which was now emphasised as the second classical language, but the language of examination was changed from Latin to Danish (Skovgaard-Petersen 1976, 88; Haue 2003, 90; Lynning 2007, 2; Olesen 2010, 8–9). With the first school law in 1814, primary schools were established and run by local communities all over the country, but these were not connected to the learned schools (Larsen *et al.* 2013, 185–188). As part of a growing political group in Denmark, farmers and landowners were eager to democratise access to further education and argued in favour of local responsibility for the learned schools. In this power struggle over the right to define and administer schools, a key issue was the purpose of education in general in society. Here the emergence of the concept of *Bildung* was a turning point. The concept of *Bildung* was introduced by the philosopher and literary critic Johann Gottfried Herder in 1774 in his ground-breaking work *Auch eine Philosophie der Geschichte zur Bildung der Menschheit* (Haue 2003). It was further developed by Immanuel Kant and implemented in the German educational system by Alexander von Humboldt and Friedrich August Wolf with the foundation of the Humboldt University in Berlin in 1810 (Held 2000; Olesen 2010).

One of the important changes this promoted in the study of classical philology was a general move from pure language studies to the study of culture, including history, geography, philosophy, mythology, art and archaeology, in what German scholarship defined as *Altertumswissenschaft*, or the scientific study of antiquity. The concept was developed as a disciplinary concept by the philologist Friedrich August Wolf (1759–1824), who is generally recognised as reforming the study of ancient languages into philology, implementing the critical reading of ancient texts as historical documents. Wolf's work is often illustrated by the anecdote of his insistence on being inscribed at the university as a student of philology, not theology, even if this study did not exist (Bolter 1980, 88; Harloe 2013, 193–202). Wolf studied in Göttingen and was a professor at the University of Halle 1783–1806; when the university closed after the Prussian defeat by Napoleon, Wolf moved to Berlin. Encouraged by Goethe, he conceptualised his many years of teaching philology in his 1807 essay "Darstellung der Alterthumswissenschaft," which can be read as a disciplinary manifesto (Bolter 1980, 84–87). In Wolf's definition of philology, three main elements distinguish the subject from previous classical scholarship. Firstly, philology is conceptualised as a professional activity reserved to an exclusive elite of researchers. Wolf opposed the popularising of research because he considered it led to superficiality. Secondly, rigorous philology, like the natural sciences, leads to the attainment of truth. Wolf was clearly influenced by developments in the natural sciences, and he reacted to the general growing awareness of them. As he states in his preface, those studying nature must recognise man as part of nature. Studies of history, language and the art of humanity are therefore to be considered knowledge of the same order as knowledge of nature (Wolf 1818, xxiv). Lastly, the goal of study was to gain knowledge of ancient humanity itself. In this view Wolf was very inspired by Humboldt and his concepts of *Bildung* and knowledge.

Wolf lays out the defining geographical borders of the subject of *Altertumswissenschaft*:

> We would like to join all these people in one science; however, there are many reasons for a necessary separation and this does not allow us to place Egyptians, Hebrews, Persians and other Oriental nations on the same level as the Greeks and Romans. One of the most important differences between them is that the first are only a few if any steps above the kind of self-realisation [*Bildung*] named bourgeois policing or civilisation, in opposition to a higher actual spiritual culture [*Geistescultur*].
>
> (Wolf 1807, 15–16)

He continues by emphasising the Greeks as the first and most original people ever to have lived on the face of the Earth, unlike the Romans, who he defines as a people of no original talents but for conquering and ruling and who built their civilisation process on that of their Greek neighbours (Wolf 1807, 22). These conceptions of Greek and Roman cultures and their interrelations owe quite a lot to the writings of Johann Joachim Winckelmann, and they underline Winckelmann's role as the "founding spirit" of *Altertumswissenschaft* and neohumanism, as these developed as a trope in German nineteenth-century narratives of the history of scholarship (Harloe 2013, 7, see also chapter 3). Wolf's conceptions also recount ancient conceptualisations of the relationship between Rome and Athens, as established already in classical literature by, for instance, Virgil (Hanink 2017, 33–34). Here is an imagined geography of Greek culture as pre-eminent above all others, which, through its originality and its qualities as role model, is embedded in the civilisation processes of Rome and then later cultures.

Wolf's concept of *Altertumswissenschaft* became very influential in Denmark. His book was translated into Danish in 1818 by Peter Oluf Brøndsted (1780–1842), professor of philology at Copenhagen University. In his preface Brøndsted emphasises how Wolf's essay nourishes and stimulates students through its high scholarly quality (Wolf 1818, viii–xiv). Brøndsted is best known for his travels in Greece and his excavations on the islands of Aegina and Kea, but he was extremely important for the implementation of Hellenism in Denmark (Christiansen 2000, 18–34; Rasmussen *et al.* 2008). He was also of paramount importance in the introduction of classical archaeology in Denmark (see chapter 4). Brøndsted became *professor extraordinarius* in philology at Copenhagen University in 1813, but he continued to travel widely as he was particularly interested in the material remains of the past. In 1832 he was made *professor ordinarius* in philology and archaeology.

In 1829, Brøndsted was joined at the University of Copenhagen by a young professor in Latin, Johan Nicolai Madvig (1804–1886). Brøndsted had paved the way for a widespread interest among the Danish intelligentsia of the early nineteenth century in the art and objects of, especially, Greece. Madvig, however, became much more influential in the educational system (Larsen 2006). Perhaps because he never travelled, unlike Brøndsted, who was constantly on the road, Madvig had a stronger position at the university. In 1848, Madvig became the first Inspector of Education at the Ministry for Education. After the passing of the constitution and the implementation of democracy in Denmark the following year, he was Minister for Church and Education from 1849 to 1851 and responsible for a new school law implemented in 1850 that increased the number of lectures in mathematics and introduced natural science into the learned schools, responding to increasing demands for skills and knowledge in these areas in society. Madvig was probably influenced by the strong voice of Hans Christian Ørsted (1777–1851), professor of physics, with whom he had implemented earlier reforms (Haue 2003, 149–152). Ørsted, who, with the realists, saw philology and the natural sciences as two very different fields, was instrumental in upgrading mathematics and natural science in the learned school (Haue 2003, 89).

Two opposing groups in nineteenth-century discussions of education and the role of the various subjects have been defined as the humanists and the realists. Conservative humanists defended the primacy of the classical languages as the most important subjects in educating pupils in universal values. Their neohumanistic theory was based on Plato's definition of the world as a materialisation of abstract ideas. Moderate humanists were more open to the expansion of *Bildung* with modern languages and natural science. The humanists were opposed by realists, who, basing themselves on Aristotle, argued that substance existed as it appeared and should be understood through the senses. The most radical realists called for the complete removal of classical languages from the school curriculum; the moderate, a reduction (Larsen 2006, 20–27; Haue 2003, 92–93).

Madvig represented a moderate wing of humanists who sought a balance between individual and general education but wished to enshrine humanity and the training of the human free spirit of the individual as the primary purpose of education (Haue 2003, 108–109). In his first year of employment, Madvig had argued in favour of the traditional neohumanist education, but in the years immediately following he began to question this, something that has been seen as a professional and a personal crisis (Larsen 2006, 18, 27–34). In his memoirs, Madvig describes as a deep frustration his feeling of a general lack of knowledge in his first years as lecturer in a course on the encyclopaedia of philology (Madvig 1887, 92–93). Coming from an ordinary background, Madvig lacked the social competences that derived from growing up in the academic milieu. He had received the general education and studied classical languages, yet he did not feel that he had succeeded in the self-realisation that was the goal of education in neohumanist ideology. Thus he questioned the unilateral formal value of language studies as promoted by Wolf, and he became instrumental in the abolition of the use of Latin as university language in examinations except in classical philology (Haue 2003, 160). In the study of Greek and Latin, he introduced a methodology of study called *autopsia*, which remains influential to this day. This was based on the formal education of studying language in depth through the original texts. In this he followed and developed the tradition into a rigorous methodology. But he clearly differed from the conservative neohumanists, who saw the classical as the ideal, as he defined Greek and Roman culture as other and primitive. The classical became a mirror in which it was possible to gain a better understanding of the present (Haue 2003, 109).

The Nordic and the classical

Madvig's school programme of 1850 was reformed in 1871 with the introduction of a two-part school system with both classical and mathematical programmes. The new system introduced an interesting novelty, the subject Old Norse (Hjorth 1972, 29–30; Haue 2003, 182–240). As described by a young contemporary theologian, the discussions about this reform were seen as widening the rift between "cis-latin" and "trans-latin": That is to say, they drew on the Latin distinction between Europe south and north of the Alps to point to a Denmark connected to Europe by the classical languages or uncoupled from it by a reduced classical content in education (Haue 2003, 196). The united liberal party had proposed a new structure with three programmes: a classical, a Nordic and a mathematical. In a speech in the upper house of parliament (*Landstinget*), Madvig argued strongly against a Nordic educational programme, seeing Danish culture as a culture developed on the borders of the civilised world and totally dependent on stimulation from Europe. If the Nordic component of education were to be strengthened, this should be done in dialogue with the European, not by focusing exclusively on the Nordic heritage (Madvig 1887, 252–253; Haue 2003, 197–198). The Nordic programme was dropped, but Old Norse was introduced as a mandatory subject for all students. The inclusion of this subject is to be understood in the context of a rising nationalism, and not least in the political changes that Denmark experienced in the 1860s (Rerup 1993). Denmark's catastrophic defeat by Prussian forces at Dybbøl Mølle in 1864 had compelled it to let go of Schleswig and the southern part of Jutland. The relationship with Germany had been problematic since the 1850s; now, anti-Germanism spread into the school system, where the aspiration to turn away from the German-inspired classical *Bildung* and the study of classical languages to a Nordic past had already been nurtured in the context of the arts in the preceding decades.

The idea of Old Norse as a Nordic alternative to the classical tradition of *Bildung* was rooted in the ideas of Grundtvig. As discussed in chapter one, Grundtvig had a formative influence on the development of Danish cultural identity in the nineteenth century and was also one of the most influential voices in the school debate.[2] He is often considered a fierce opponent of the classical tradition and is known as a very strong agitator for the abolition of what he called "the black school," referring to the learned schools in which grammar was studied intensively for its own sake. However, Grundtvig himself had received a classical education, graduating in theology from the University of Copenhagen in 1803. What set him apart from earlier thinkers in Denmark was his focus on education for the people, together with an idea of the Enlightenment inspired by Herder's thinking – that there are as many Enlightenments as people and individuals (Jonas 2014). In this respect Grundtvig opposed the privileged position of the classical cultures in traditional education. His clash with Madvig came when he proposed that the Academy of Sorø be reconstituted as a high school focused on "Danishness," something that Madvig refused, arguing that both the learned schools and the university were teaching the spirit of Danishness (Lundgreen-Nielsen 1993, 262). Grundtvig, in reply, called Madvig the Latin minister, obliged like a rigid Latinist to consider all non-Greek and non-Roman civilisations as barbarian (Grundtvig 1848).

In 1889, the Ministry of Education published a proposal for a reform of the upper secondary school and asked the schools to comment. A key element was the abolition of two subjects, Old Norse and ancient Greek, to make room for more lectures in Latin and mathematics. Most in fact agreed that Old Norse was not that important: The subject introduced a new and difficult grammar, and there were not enough lectures for the students to really get to the content of Icelandic literature and the sagas. Those against the proposal argued that all young male students should get to know the literature and spirit of the Nordic past and that a knowledge of Old Norse was important for understanding the mother tongue (Kirke-og Undervisningsministeriet 1889, 16–17, 52). It was different with the suggested abolition of ancient Greek. The school principals in general agreed that knowledge of Greek culture was absolutely necessary and an essential part of the general education. A few argued that this knowledge should be obtained through reading the original texts,[3] but there were several who supported the Ministry of Education's proposal that it should be acquired by reading Greek literature in translation. In these arguments, some of the tropes concerning the role of Greek culture that would be repeated in the years to come were formulated:

• Greek culture embodies a liberating force, as exemplified firstly through the case of Rome (which cultivated the culture of the conquered, then spread it through Latin literature and art and thereby established the common culture of Western Europe) and secondly through the Renaissance (when the rediscovery of classical texts was essential in breaking with mediaeval tradition and culture: Kirke-og Undervisningsministeriet 1889, 21)
• A civilised country has citizens who know ancient Greek. Not knowing Greek culture means a loss of civilisation (Kirke-og Undervisningsministeriet 1889, 63)
• Knowledge of the classical past, and especially of Greek culture, is essential to the understanding of modern European cultural life, of which Denmark is part (Kirke-og Undervisningsministeriet 1889, 63)

Ancient Greek was considered the most important discipline in general education and self-realisation. Old Norse was considered more of a skill, necessary for those studying the Danish language. It is astonishing that Old Norse was so easily dismissed, but this fact underlines the classical background of all teachers of the subject. The argument that established ancient Greek culture as the essential discipline for all students was that Greek culture was essential for the understanding of the values and structures not only of Danish but of European societies. It was the outlook and the connection with Europe that set the subject apart from Old Norse, which located Danish culture in a Nordic sphere. Thus, in the imagined geography of classicism, Greek culture was the link between Denmark and Europe.

The invention of Classical Studies

When the school reform was finally decided in 1903, it was a breakthrough in several respects. It merged the various different schools into one educational system in which primary school was followed by four years in the intermediate school and then three years in upper secondary school, now called the gymnasium (Skovgaard-Petersen 1976; Haue 2003; Gjerløff and Jacobsen 2014).[4] The name *gymnasium* had been used since the 1620s by a few Danish schools offering a two-year preparation for university. The term derives from the Greek word referring to the institution for training the minds and especially the bodies of young men in ancient Greece. During the Renaissance, the term had been appropriated for higher education by the humanists, but it was only now introduced as defining upper secondary school in Denmark with the 1903 reform, clearly inspired by Germany, where the term had been institutionalised by Humboldt in 1812 as the unitarian name for schools providing access to university studies (Horster and Funder 2017). The reform provided for girls to be admitted to upper secondary school. The school was divided into three programmes: modern languages, classical languages, and mathematics. Latin was still taught in all classes, and students choosing the classical programme were to take ancient Greek, but Classical Studies as proposed in 1889 became mandatory for all students, prescribing one hour a week throughout all three years of the educational programme.

Classical Studies was a new subject, with no tradition and no formal education of teachers. Martin Clarentius Gertz, a professor in philology, was appointed by the ministry to draw up the statutory instrument on the content of teaching, based on suggestions from a number of committees. His draft was followed in all its detail: "Among the Greek authors should be read parts of Homer, at least two dramas and examples of Plato and other prosaic authors. To this should be added – though less – examples of Latin key authors."[5] In the end, the reading of Latin authors was very seldom included, and in 1953 this requirement was removed from the guidelines (Andersen 2000, 66, 73).

Two elements introduced at the very beginning are still essential in the methodological and theoretical approach: the methodology of *autopsia* in learning, and the quality of the texts or monuments as normative for European culture. *Autopsia* (seeing with one's own eyes) derived from the philological methods introduced by Madvig. Originally, learning by seeing firsthand had been based on reading the original texts. This was now transferred into a conceptualisation of the text as a whole as a monument, comparable to the sculptures, temples and vases studied by students. This was not detailed engagement with the grammar of words and sentences, but reading of the content of primary texts as opposed to secondary literature.[6] This methodology is still characterised as a special method for the subject in Danish upper secondary schools, and it differentiates Classical Studies from similar studies such as history or history of religion. It is a rather positivistic approach, defined by one of the teachers as "through seeing yourself and on a documentary basis the students gain an authentic image of a culture" (Bender *et al*. 1981, 32; Krarup 1953, 11–12). The choice of methodology for the new subject followed from the teachers' training as philologists. They were thus applying the methods that they had learned and practised when reading the texts in Greek.

In 1953, the Greek and Latin teacher Per Krarup described the philologist teaching with translations as "gasping for air like a fish on dry land" – clearly not in his element, and almost embarrassed by having to talk about the texts without going back to the original Greek texts (Krarup 1953, 15). Nothing in philological university studies prepared these teachers for teaching in translation. Teachers of Greek and Latin in the upper secondary schools were still clearly the most qualified, but the need for more teachers consequently opened up the subject so that historians and teachers of literature, history, religion and Danish could teach Classical Studies. For a short period in the 1950s and 1960s, the University of Copenhagen offered a course in Greek culture (Krarup 1953, 16). However, a university degree was developed only in 1980 at Aarhus and Odense universities, encouraged by the Classical Association (Oldtidskundskab 1981).

One obstacle was the availability of translations. In the first place, only authors already translated could be taught, a consideration used as an argument against the subject in the first place. A society for the translation of historical sources had been established in 1875, and Gertz himself had founded a series called "Greek and Latin authors" in 1901, both initiatives that intensified the production of translations (Afzelius 1950, 137; Andersen 2000, 67). As late as 1947, the classical philologist Thure Hastrup was complaining about the lack of high-quality translations of essential texts (Hastrup 1947, 380). He emphasised the translations of Homer's *Iliad* and *Odyssey* excellently done by Christian Wilster in the 1830s (Krarup 1953, 12). These were reissued several times and used for teaching until new translations were published by Otto Steen Due in 2002 and 2004 respectively. But of Aristotle, for instance, very few translations existed, and only much later were many of the Aristotelian texts made available in Danish. It is informative to look at what was translated in the first years after the reform, and here the three tragedians are used as illustrative examples (Table 2.1).[7] A number of translations of Aeschylus and Euripides had been made in the first half of the nineteenth century, although Hastrup considered only those by Niels Møller really qualified. He had translated three plays by Aischylos: *The Agamemnon* in 1891 (reissued in 1966), *The Eumenides* in 1904 and *The Persians* in 1918.

There were very few plays by Sophocles in Danish, although *Antigone* had been translated by Thor Lange in 1893 and Niels Møller in 1894, with both these translations reissued several times until the 1960s, when

Table 2.1 Translations of tragedies by Aeschylus, Sophocles and Euripides into Danish. Those emphasised in bold have been reissued several times

	Translations available in 1903	Translations made 1903–1949	Translations made after 1950
Aischylos	**Agamemnon** 1790, 1819, 1820,1842, **1891**	**1911**	1966, 1974, 1980, 2007
	Choephorae 1805, 1820, 1844	**1904, 1915**, 1933	1989, 2007
	Eumenides 1821, 1844	**1918**	1991, 2007
	The Persians 1854		
	Prometheus 1854, 1869		1957, 1975
	Seven Against Thebes 1854		2012
	The Supplicants 1854		
Sophocles	Ajax	**1903**	1991
	Antigone 1797, **1893, 1894**		1959, 1966, 1977, 1983, 2004
	Electra 1797, 1884	1912	1986, 1988
	Oedipus at Colonus		1963, 1988
	Oedipus the King **1897**		1958, 1977, 1990, 2017
	Philoctetes		1964, 1997, 2016
	Women of Trachis		2014

(Continued)

Table 2.1 (Continued)

	Translations available in 1903	Translations made 1903–1949	Translations made after 1950
Euripides	Alcestis 1840	1913	2010
	Andromache 1840		2004
	Bacchae 1840	1931	1966, 1985
	Cyclops 1820, 1875		1988
	Electra 1875		1963
	Hecuba 1840		1996
	Children of Heracles 1875		
	Madness of Heracles 1875		
	Helen 1875		1985
	Hippolytus 1840	1913	1951, 1958, 1966, 2013
	Hypsipyle	1914	
	Ion 1875	1911	1997
	Iphigenia at Aulis 1840	1914	1975, 1982
	Iphigenia among the Taurians 1840		1982, 2001
	Medea 1840	1911	1954, 1973, 1986, 2016
	Orestes 1875		2009
	Phoenician Women 1875		1998
	Rhesus 1875		1976
	Suppliants 1875		
	Trojan Women 1868–1869		1992

the first new translations appeared (Andersen 2000). It is rather astonishing that the new subject did not provoke more new translations and that many of the works translated in the early years of the century did not become key texts in teaching. The plays used again and again were Aischylos's *Agamemnon* and *The Persians*, Sophocles's *Antigone* and Euripides's *Medea*, this last in spite of complaints about the quality of existing translations. As new translations appeared in the 1970s, Aeschylus seems to have been superseded by Euripides (Krarup 1953, 13; Andersen 2000, 83). Clearly, these plays are also those most favoured by more recent translators. Some translations were made for new performances, with especially *Antigone* and *Medea* being popular. It seems to have been difficult to widen the repertoire of the canonical texts once this was first established. A change came in the 1970s, when the Classical Association sponsored a series of translations including a large number of new translations that were made available for teachers and schools at reasonable prices (Andersen 2000).

Although *autopsia* rendered the use of readers or textbooks unnecessary, introductions to Greek literature to be used in teaching the subject appeared rather soon anyway. One of the first was published in 1912 by Valdemar Nielsen (Nielsen 1912). It is an interesting document, as it provides us with an insight into the contextualisation of the textual material. The book was reprinted several times, most recently in 1966. Nielsen provides a framework for understanding the texts in the context of an ancient society, focusing on the authors and their personalities. For instance, the Aeolians are described as the most energetic and bold people with an unrestrained passion demanding satisfaction, and he considers this as a "national dowry" which accounted for the emergence of poets such as Sappho and Alcaeus. The reader also provides us with the framework for the canon of text established in this period. It begins with Homer's *Iliad* and *Odyssey*, followed by Hesiod, who is credited not for writing interesting literature but for being the first named individual person in European literature (Nielsen 1912, 6). Then come the poets – Tyrtaeus, Solon, Alcaeus, Sappho, Anacreon, Simonides and Pindar – to be followed by the three great tragedians, Aeschylus, Sophocles and Euripides. Aristophanes and, in brief, Menander are mentioned as authors of comedies. The presentation of the authors is framed by information about the oral and musical performances of lyric and the development and physical scenography of the dramas. The historians, Herodotus and Thucydides, are presented with an evaluation of their personality. Herodotus is presented as a naive and credulous man, more storyteller than historian, whereas Thucydides is the exact opposite, critical of superstition and shaped by the liberal environment of Athens of his time. Xenophon is described as dry and less spirited, and he is condemned for his preference for Sparta that prevents him from giving the Athenians their due praise. Lastly, the philosophers are presented: first the pre-Socratics such as Thales of Miletus, then Pythagoras, Anaxagoras and Democritos. The sophists are discussed at greater length and depth. The sections on Protagoras, Socrates, Plato and Aristotle focus on their philosophical ideas, but Socrates in particular is also delineated through anecdotes like the one when his wife poured a jug of water over his head when he tried to leave after being scolded, after which he then calmly noted that after thunder comes rain (Nielsen 1912, 26).[8] The choice to include an anecdote that is not appearing in the original texts and is only preserved in later commentaries, but at the same time one repeated again and again, could be a didactic choice. On the other hand, it goes into the more popularising genre that we saw Wolf condemning 100 years earlier. The short chapter on rhetoric focuses on a detailed presentation of Demosthenes as the defender of Athenian greatness, and it laments the widespread demoralisation and weakness in Athens (Nielsen 1912, 34). The book ends with a very short piece on later philosophy and the Roman period: "In the Roman period it is Greek *Bildung* that has given the Roman its character" (Nielsen 1912, 37).

Nielsen's reader follows the teaching process itself. From 1903, students took the subject for three years. Eventually a hierarchy was established whereby in the first year they read Homer and in the second, the tragedies; only in the third year were they mature enough to read philosophy (Krarup 1953, 12–14). The curriculum was defined as at least 3,000 lines of Homer, one drama, 150 pages of prose, and 50 pages from Latin authors. This turned out to be too much, and in 1922 it was reduced to 2,000 lines of Homer, two tragedies, and 125 pages of prose, half of which was to be Plato and the remainder drawn from the historians. Teachers could read 25 pages of Latin authors, but this was seldom done, and this option as removed in 1953 (Andersen 2000, 73). The peripheral role of Latin was counteracted by a new act in 1971 which added *Roman* in parentheses every time *Greek* was mentioned – a rather subtle attempt to include Latin and Roman literature (Bekendtgørelse 1971, §11). The parentheses were removed in a new act in 1987, under which the focus was defined as classical Athenian literature, with the option of including texts from earlier and later periods if they were deemed to contribute to learning (Undervisningsministeriet 1988, §23). In other respects, the content remained the same and was only changed in 2002 with the addition of the study of the later reception, as will be discussed further below. But, first, it is necessary to look at the different challenges that produced the twentieth century's legitimatising arguments or tropes, which led to this change of content.

Challenging Classical Studies

The mandatory status of Classical Studies has been challenged several times since its inception. In the mid-1930s and again in the mid-1940s, it was suggested that Classical Studies be substituted by a new subject, Contemporary Studies. In 1958 and again in the 1970s, it had been suggested that Classical Studies be made optional (Haue 2003, 339–341, 349, 368, 386–387). Even in the 1930s, students felt the subject to be of little value for their education (Haue 2003, 349). In the mid-1980s, a report on the teaching of humanistic subjects in secondary school suggested that Classical Studies be abolished and integrated partly in a new subject called Religion – philosophy, partly in the subjects of history and literature studies. Once again, however, Classical Studies survived, and even gained in strength when teaching was moved to the last of the three years of the secondary school programme and taught three hours per week (Haue 2003, 498; Undervisningsministeriet 1988; Bolt-Jørgensen *et al.* 1985).[9] At the turn of the millennium, in a context of major societal change, the educational system was scrutinised once again. This time, a new subject, Cultural Studies (*kulturfag*), was suggested. It was argued that Classical Studies in its present form had outlived its usefulness, because Latin had at this point been so reduced that students were lacking what they had achieved in Latin previously (Undervisningsministeriet 1997; Bolt-Jørgensen *et al.* 2003; Zibrandtsen 2003). The idea was not implemented because, among other reasons, the Danish Peoples Party questioned this change (Frevert 2003). Instead, the content demands for Classical Studies were reformed by adding a new dimension, that of "perspective" or reception, with the mandatory inclusion of Latin authors. This change was fundamental. Classical Studies was now no longer studied with the main focus of knowing the classical past as an essential part of our common heritage, but instead to understand the later use and meaning of this particular past. This was a new way of legitimising the relevance of the subject, moving the focus to the afterlife of the classical past and its role in European history and culture.

It is quite impressive how Classical Studies as a rather small subject in the curriculum has been able to survive the modernisation processes of the upper secondary school. The arguments carried forward during the various crises that have confronted Classical Studies are embedded in the tropes that have developed out of discussions since the nineteenth century. The question of the role of Classical Studies in the general education offered by Danish secondary schools provoked a number of publications, even *apologiae*, in 1981 (Bender 1981), 1985 (Bolt-Jørgensen *et al.* 1985) and 2003 (Bolt-Jørgensen *et al.* 2003; Andreasen 2003). These four volumes include comments and reflections not only from teachers and professors, but also from journalists, authors, actors and other representatives of Danish society invited to demonstrate how learning Greek and Latin or Classical Studies has been essential to their personal and career development and for society as a whole. Three of these volumes were published by the Classical

Association (*Klassikerforeningen*), founded around 1935, which has been a very strong advocate for Classical Studies and of paramount importance to its development and survival (Iuul 1985). One of the goals of the Classical Association was the exchange of information, and its membership magazine, founded in 1967 with a first issue of only one page, has developed into a lively forum for discussion, with articles spanning texts, teaching, art, politics and all themes related to the Latin, Greek and Classical Studies in upper secondary school.[10] The association has also been responsible for further education, study tours, and European cooperation. The following analysis of the tropes that have emerged in discussions of the subject is based on the four publications referred to above, although a lively discussion has also been taking place in the Classical Association's membership magazine and in public media.[11]

First trope: Greek antiquity is alive

One of the major criticisms of spending many teaching hours on ancient Greek and Latin has been the fact that the languages are no longer spoken. They are "dead languages" which have no practical use in present-day society, as students argued in 1933. Wolf had already been confronted with this argument in the eighteenth century as natural sciences and a general turn towards more utilitarian subjects began to influence universities through the ideas of Rousseau (Bolter 1980, 88–89). The argument for maintaining Greek culture as essential in Danish education turns this around. The argument says that because the Greeks created a culture that shaped Western minds and civilisation, we are all Greeks, and we all speak Greek (Wivel 1985, 9; Gjørup 2003, 15; Mejer 2003, 81). This is the strongest legitimation, and it has been carried forward through all discussions.

The argument is made on two levels in the Danish discourse. One is the overall societal level. Here it is argued that European language and civil society were shaped by the classical Greek period, so it is essential to know this period in order to understand ourselves and the world around us. To quote Hans Hauge, former professor of Danish and English literature:

> How many Greek and Latin words have I not already used after so few words? Philosophy thinks in Greek, as Derrida had said: there is thus no philosophy that is not "Greek". Our literature is Greek. No one opens the mouth about that without speaking Greek.
>
> (Hauge 2003, 284)

This argument is based on an approach to language as fundamental and essential for human social culture, organisation and thinking. It is based on Herder's theory of peoples as ethnic groups and exemplified in Shelley's famous quote, "We are all Greeks" (Olesen 2010, 4). It also carries an embedded imperialism and elitism. As Simon Goldhill has remarked on Victorian Britain:

> Part of the justification of the continuing study of classics was that it formed, as well as informed, the mind, and formed the mind not just for the gentleman, but for a figure of authority. A training in how to rule.
>
> (Goldhill 2011, 2)

In fact, to "We are all Greeks" has often been added "except the Greeks," thus implying the appropriation by the Western world of Greek culture (Pelt 2000, 31, 40).

The other level of argument in this trope focuses more directly on scholarship, stressing the necessity of knowing Greek and Latin in order to do research within a number of areas. Typically, this argument is used by scholars from other disciplines (Andersen 1985, 48–49; Bager 1985, 86; Windfeld 1985, 97). On the one hand, the entire conceptualisation of Western scholarship is based on ancient sources such as Plato and Aristotle (Pade 2003; Thomsen 2003; Tortzen 2003; Wagner 2003; Zeeberg 2003). On the other, the actual use of Greek and Latin – especially Latin – by European elites in the arts and sciences until the eighteenth century, when national languages began to win ground in writing and teaching, makes researching history impossible without knowledge of Latin. This argument not only is applicable to Classical Studies but is advanced to advocate the preservation of Greek and Latin as languages.

Second trope: Greek antiquity is civilisation

The belief that we are shaped by the Greek mind and the Greek spirit is related to the definition of the Greeks as the first civilisation. The key word here is *roots* (in Danish, *rødder*). Ancient Greek culture is defined as the *roots* of European culture:

> Where are my roots? In Klim in Vester Hanherred, if this is where my great grandfather guarded his sheeps, of course yes, if you talk about genealogy, but if it is about linguistic awareness and common ideas about values, the answer is completely different. Here we find the roots in Athens, Jerusalem and Rome.
>
> (Bolt-Jørgensen 2003, 7–8)

Here the imagined geography is very clearly defined as a mental and sociological community based on common ideas and values. Several authors locate the roots in Athens, Jerusalem and Rome, but Athens has a special place as the origin of these roots (Bender et. al. 1981, 18; Kaarstad 1985, 45; Jansen 1985, 51; Tamm 2003). The theologian and philosopher Johannes Sløk (1916–2001) even defines Hellas and Athens as the authentic roots, whereas the other important roots – Jewish culture and Christianity – are latecomers (Sløk 1985, 16). The Greeks shaped a world of arts, literature, democracy and freedom, and without these elements, a society cannot be defined as a civilisation. This also means that marginalising the classical past would be catastrophic. With no knowledge of the Greek past, we will be rootless, and we will end up not being civilised (Wulf-Jørgensen 1985, 68; Høeg 2003, 16).

It is also frequently stated that the surviving texts of the Greek philosophers and writers cover a range of themes that are still essential today in order to discuss a broad range of subjects in class, and that no other culture is capable of providing this material – and even if they were, it would then be necessary to go back to the Greek authors in order to understand them fully (Hansen 1985, 93; Johansen 1985b 28–29). This is a legacy of the philological traditions developed by Wolf in his *Darstellung der Alterthumswissenschaften*, where he argues that the Greeks cannot be compared to other ancient cultures because the Greeks simply had reached a higher intellectual level (Wolf 1818; Hanink 2017, 115–116).

Third trope: Greek antiquity is liberation

When the classical is defined as civilisation, this also implies a possibility of using the classical as a model, a possibility of returning to civilisation when development has been proceeding in a wrong direction. Whenever European culture has seen the need to renew itself, it has turned to the classical cultures. This was the case in the Renaissance in Italy, and in the Enlightenment (Høeg 2003). It is a key element in the concept of classicism that depends on a circular temporality implementing a rebirth after death, as discussed earlier. With Hellenism, Greek classical culture in particular has come to exemplify a special concept of freedom and liberty that has been incorporated into the idea of a special Western culture. As one teacher of Classical Studies has expressed it: "Classical Studies has to show how the archaic human being broke from mythos to logos – to show how free thoughts created free people" (Galmar 1985, 88).

For the journalist Peter Wivel, this position is exemplified by the East German author Christa Wolf, who in her novel *Kassandra* "speaks Greek," figuratively speaking, using the "language of the past" – the mythological arena of the war between Greeks and Trojans – as the only language available to her to maintain a connection with civilisation, separated as she is by the division of Europe (Wivel 1985, 9–10). Wolf's novel was written before the fall of the Berlin Wall and the end of the Cold War, thus illustrating how ancient Greek texts were used as a liberating tool of expression.

Fourth trope: Roman antiquity is the first classicism

In Classical Studies, Greek culture was the primary subject. As the twentieth century progressed, however, Latin and Roman authors became more included in the curriculum: At first their works were optional, but since 2002 they have become a mandatory element. However, many of the discussions present Roman art as a reception of Greek art (Gjørup 2003, 18–19; Thomsen 2005, 10; Høeg 2003, 15). The Augustan period is particularly emphasised as the most relevant, focusing on Virgil and a classicising artistic style. The same trope is also evident in many of the later textbooks produced in the course of the twentieth century (for instance, Fich *et al.* 1999, 288).

Scholars have identified a quite denigratory attitude towards Roman culture. This has been explained as a Danish anti-Romanism developed in the late nineteenth century as part of Grundtvig's critique of the black or learned schools and the rise of Hellenism that was clearly much more marked in Denmark than in Sweden (Carlsen 2003, 29; Elkjær and Krarup 1947, 18; Lundgreen-Nielsen 1993). The Rome pictured by Danish poets and writers is peopled by distant, cold, weak, degenerate, heartless, brutal, slanderous, irreligious and perverted seekers after power – the most positive to be said is that they were stout and disciplined pragmaticists.

Fifth trope: Greek heritage is shared European heritage

An essential part of the legitimation of Classical Studies since its inception has been the connection to Europe, as we have seen above. This idea of Greek culture as European culture grew even stronger in the course of the twentieth century, as will be made evident in the following section. The philologist Jørgen Meyer argued in 2003 that Greek, Latin and Classical Studies are a necessity for students in order to understand their own past, and "that these give Europe a community and a feeling of belonging that is important if the European Union is to develop into a superpower in a world of superpowers" (Mejer 2003, 83). Here again, the classical subjects are a key element in the Danish accession to the imagined community of Europe. Other discourses talk about "a common European background" (Bolt-Jørgensen *et al.* 1981, 26; Johansen 1985a, 44), "how the European human was shaped" (Johansen 1985b, 28), and ancient texts as "tangible cultural heritage that makes Denmark not only a province but also a part of Europe" (Petersen 1985, 75). In this sense the future of Europe is dependent on the survival of the ancient Greek and Latin languages and knowledge of

Greek and Roman culture. It is only through this prism that Danes are able to recognise themselves as Europeans.

Classical Studies as European heritage

The arguments embedded particularly in the last of the five tropes outlined above paved the way for a change in the identity and content of Classical Studies in 2003. The concept of Europe had been increasingly used since the 1980s as an argument for the importance of the subject, having been an essential component in the discourse on the Nordic/Danish and the Greek/European. Since the 1980s, there has been a change in the discourse, with the focus changing from general education to an ideological legitimation of Classical Studies. It had to be relevant to contemporary life, and this was argued through the increasing importance of Europe in contemporary Denmark, as the concept of Europe has changed in train with the development of the European Union.

The Danish-European connection during this period has not been straightforward. After Denmark joined the EU in 1973, participation was followed by scepticism about the role and influence of the EU. However, that Denmark was the only Nordic country to join the EU at this time underlines its special connection with Europe among the Nordic countries (Hansen 2002. Sweden and Finland joined in 1995). Denmark defined this step as a bridging between the Nordic and the European, but it has since become a political balancing act between participation and hesitation, as expressed through a number of referendums whenever the EU moved towards closer integration, leading to the Danish amendments and the decision not to join the European Monetary Union in 2000.

In the consolidating act of 1987, the European connection was for the first time specified as essential for the purpose of student learning: "that the students through the knowledge of Greek culture acquire common European conceptualisation and idioms in order to understand and be able to relate their own society" (Undervisningsministeriet 1988, 407). The expanded teaching guidelines specified how the knowledge of Greek culture is a tool with which to understand contemporary society and a shared European mentality. The word used is *code* – Greek culture is a code that you need to know to fully understand the underlying meaning of Danish and European culture (Undervisningsministeriet 1988, 408). The same word was used again by classical scholar Sten Ebbesen when he defended Greek as a university subject in 2015, when the University of Copenhagen considered to close it down (Ebbesen 2016). It is a word that underlines the normative character of the subject. The arguments in the *apologiae* discussed above talk about the "key to understanding our society" (Bender et al. 1981, 3;

Bolt-Jørgensen 2003, 10). The implication is that without this key or code, it is impossible to manoeuvre in present-day society.

The reform of 2002 had serious consequences for Classical Studies, because Latin was removed as a mandatory independent subject and integrated with a subject called general language understanding (*almen sprog-forståelse*). This strengthened the need for Latin and Roman literature to be included in Classical Studies, and thus two major changes were made: the reading of at least one Latin author and the inclusion of "perspective," something that could be presented as the reception of antiquity but, as will be shown below, has a slightly different meaning. The relevance of the discipline was thus transformed into a methodological practice with which students had to analyse the use of ancient ideas, concepts and art forms in later European culture. The guideline introduced the paragraph on identity before the one on purpose and the change in focus is spelt out:

> Classical Studies is a cultural discipline about antiquity as the basis for European culture. The discipline concerns ancient texts and monuments in which values, concepts and forms that became norms in European culture, are expressed.
>
> (Stx-bekendtgørelsen 2004, bilag 45)

Since the change of 2003, it has been stated that this turn to the normative role of European culture through the study of perspective has secured the survival of Classical Studies as an independent subject. It has been argued that without its rich afterlife in European history, the classical cultures would probably occupy the same place in upper secondary high school as Egyptology, Nordic mythology or the Renaissance – which is to say none (Jørgensen *et al.* 2014, 4). This is in clear opposition to the trope defining classical culture as civilisation and stating that no other culture had attained the level of the classical and thus of Western civilisation. This change therefore represents an attempt to rethink the premise and meaning of the subject of Classical Studies by including the idea of perspective and by challenging the constructed privileged position of Greek culture. As discussed in chapter 1, reception studies have boomed in recent decades, and a number of new and innovative studies have focused attention on the nineteenth century's problematic conceptualisation of the classical past. Thus the reform of 2002 opened up the space for these elements to be introduced into teaching.

However, in the ministry's teaching guidelines, the engagement with perspective is consistently defined as working with the traces from classical antiquity that can be seen, firstly, in the continuing influence on language and, secondly, in the unique "repeated return to the origin in classical antiquity in marked periods of liberation in Western civilisation – for instance in the

Renaissance and the Enlightenment" (Undervisningsministeriet 2010, 3–4; Stx-læreplaner 2017, 3). This is a reversion to the arguments we encountered above, characterising Greek culture as still alive and as liberation. There is no attempt here to go deeper into the construction of these tropes to develop this into more critical studies of reception. In fact, the definitions seem to point to consolidating the normative rather than questioning it. Later in the guidelines, the recovery of the traces is described as revealing "the key to the understanding of essential elements of European culture and knowledge about our own identity" (Undervisningsministeriet 2010, 4). Once again we meet the metaphor of paving the way for understanding.

The authors of a 2014 report on perspective in teaching suggest a new line of enquiry through a focus on the non-homogeneous in the ancient texts, looking at pairs of opposites such as friend/enemy, individual/community (Jørgensen *et al.* 2014, 13–14). Here, the critical perspectives are embedded in a questioning of who defines and authorises the discourse of the universal. In an anthology published in 2005 to act as inspiration for the teacher in navigating this new minefield, philologist Ole Thomsen presents perhaps the most critical text on classical heritage in this context, turning his attention to a number of the established discourses on how Greek culture was sustained through Roman reception so as to develop what has been defined as the Graeco-Roman unified culture. He challenges the traditional approach – that we study the classical because it has made us who we are – by explaining it as naive or self-assertive, and by applying a multicultural perspective which questions how the Greeks were appropriated to make Western culture what it is and what negative consequences this might have had (Thomsen 2005, 9–16). Critical thinking is at the core of the goal of teaching, and it has been argued many times that the Greek texts provide excellent material with which to learn critical reflection (Stx-lærerplaner 2017, 4–6). Still, this kind of critical investigation is nearly absent from the ministry's teaching guidelines.

The discourses in Denmark concerning Classical Studies have until now reflected the general European appropriation of classical cultures as global heritage belonging to us all (Petersen 1985, 71). These discourses continue to pursue what has recently been defined, in a reinterpretation of the history of classical reception, as the colonisation of the classical (Hanink 2017). Classical heritage has been conceptualised as a universal heritage, shared by all European nations. In the most recent reform of upper secondary school in 2017, the identity of Classical Studies has now acquired a global dimension: "Classical Studies is a knowledge, information and culture subject that addresses antiquity as the basis of art and imagination in later periods in Europe as well as globally."[12]

The subject of Classical Studies is now confronted by the new demand that the European dimension be extended to a global dimension. This development was not generated by a globalising approach to Classical Studies, but specified in the political agreement between the government and the parties supporting the reform, with the objective of strengthening global competences and cultural understanding through the use and understanding of languages.[13] Hans Hauge prophesied a revival of the classical tradition already in 2003, when he entitled an article in one of the apologias to which I have referred as "Classical Studies is Globalisation." He argued that the classical would return as the essential in general education, because nationalism was on its way out: That nationalism and the focus on national cultures were a parenthesis in the *longue durée* and that the classical tradition was returning, as it was this that had been the Danish connection to the world beyond our borders (Hauge 2003). Thus, the imagined geography of classicism was reborn. The role of classicism on a global scale has, as mentioned in the introduction, recently been subjected to postcolonial critique, but this dimension is totally absent from the ministerial guidelines.

The Victory of Hellenism

The continued vitality of Classical Studies can be interpreted as the victory of Hellenism in Denmark. The subject has survived for more than 100 years and has changed its rationale from general education and self-realisation to more and more weight being laid on utilitarian skills. In spite of this, Classical Studies has survived due to its slow transformation from being primarily a study of language to a literary subject, until today it has become a cultural study. This progression has sustained the role of classical culture as the link between a Nordic and a European sphere in a shifting political environment. The content of the subject continues to give priority to the Greek classical period, thus defining the role of the classical past in the spirit of Hellenism.

The reason for the survival of Classical Studies as a secondary school subject in Denmark as compared to Norway and Sweden is surely this link between Denmark and Europe at the time of Danish participation in the EU – even if this last has met with scepticism and hesitation. Studying Greek and Roman culture rather than Greek and Roman languages has proved to be a way of keeping a bond with a historical past whose relevance on the border of Europe has been contested and challenged.

Whereas Classical Studies is still considered essential to a historical understanding of present society, Latin has suffered, and in fact has almost been abolished as mandatory. Latin was never studied as a cultural subject but was predominantly considered a language subject. The elimination of Latin from the Danish educational system is part of a general language crisis in Denmark, in which also many modern languages are now highly endangered both as subjects in upper secondary schools and as university subjects. Even if Danes in general master more than their native language (normally

English) and understand other Nordic languages, there has been a steep decline in the number of students studying foreign languages in the *gymnasium* as well as in further education. The decline of Greek and Latin as languages is part of this development.

Notes

1 The numbers derive from Statistics Denmark, published annual reports 1910–2004 and their digital database from 2004: www.dst.dk/en (accessed 24 June 2018).

2 Grundtvig's collected works are digitised and made available through the research centre the Grundtvig Study Centre (Grundtvigcenteret) at Aarhus University; see http://grundtvigcenteret.au.dk (accessed 18 March 2018).

3 This is strongly argued by the philologist Johan Ludvig Heiberg (1854–1928). See Forhandlinger (1889, 28–33), also published in Heiberg (1889).

4 Many of the schoolmasters proposed a postponement of the reform, and there was no political will to change the system before, early in the twentieth century, a change of government in 1901 eventually brought the liberal party Venstre to power (Haue 2003). The new minister of education, J. C. Christensen, and the head of education, Martin Cl. Gertz, succeeded in passing the law in 1903, and the new structure began to be implemented in autumn 1907 (Andersen 2000, 66).

5 Bekendtgørelse om Undervisning i gymnasiet 1906, 4.12.

6 Bolt-Jørgensen (2003, 8–9). Whether this methodology is equivalent when studying translations was also discussed. Those arguing in favour of keeping the Greek language clearly rejected this; see Scharling (1903, 38–41).

7 The information derives from the online bibliography *Oldtidens og Middelalders litteratur – I skandinaviske oversættelser* by Johanna Akujärvi and Lars Boje Mortensen: http://skandinaviske-oversaettelser.net/da/ (accessed 11 April 2018).

8 There are different versions of the anecdote, and describing the jug as a water jug is a rather innocent version, as others mention a chamber pot.

9 Haue (2003, 482, 485–486). Rapport om de humanistiske fag 1985. It is quite astonishing that there were no philologists in the group appointed by the ministry to write the report, and it is difficult not to see this as the reason for the ease with which the abolition of Classical Studies was suggested, even if all agreed that it incorporated all the essential elements of general education that were the key goal of the education, as argued by the group.

10 See the homepage: www.klassikerforeningen.dk (accessed 11 April 2018). The history of the association has never been written. A short summary of the first 50 years was published in the journal by the chairman Christian Iuul in 1985, but there are no archives from the first 30 years of its existence.

11 On the occasion of the debates in the 1970s, the editor of the membership magazine published a list of media appearances.

12 Læreplan for oldtidskundskab 2017: https://uvm.dk/-/media/filer/uvm/gym-laereplaner-2017/stx/oldtidskundskab-c-stx-august-2017.pdf?la=da (accessed 25 February 2018).

13 Aftale mellem regeringen, Socialdemokraterne, Dansk Folkeparti, Liberal Alliance, Det Radikale Venstre, Socialistisk Folkeparti og Det Konservative Folkeparti om styrkede gymnasiale uddannelser, 16 June 2016: www.uvm.dk/-/media/filer/uvm/udd/gym/pdf16/jun/160603-styrkede-gymnasiale-uddannelser.pdf (25 February 2018), 21–22.

3   The imagined geographies of collecting

Displaying classical antiquity in Danish museums

This chapter explores how Danish museums' exhibiting of classical material culture conceptualises Denmark and Danish identity within the European cultural landscape. It concentrates on two museums in particular, the National Museum of Denmark and the Ny Carlsberg Glyptotek. Not only do these two institutions host the largest and most important collections of classical antiquities in Denmark, they also offer a continuous sequence of engagement with the material culture of classical antiquity in Denmark, stretching back to the beginning of the nineteenth century. The exhibitions reflect the history of the museum institution that houses them and the mutating conceptualisations of their classical collections in a national and European perspective. Although this chapter will also touch on perspectival material shown in older exhibitions, it will focus on the formation of the museums' collections and their most recent exhibitions in order to assess continuities and breaks in the ideological conceptualisation of classical antiquity as part of a Danish imagined geography.[1]

Before we turn our attention to the Danish context, a short excursion into the history of exhibitions of classical antiquities in Europe from the late eighteenth century up until the present will illuminate two central schisms in the interpretation and dissemination of classical antiquity: firstly, the dialectics between an art historical and an archaeological approach; and, secondly, the ongoing discussion of the meaning of context as an essentially epistemological concept in the narratives created in the exhibitions. We will pay special attention to how these concepts tie in with notions of geography and how geographical concepts have developed in the history of classical collections and museum exhibitions.

Classicism and collecting

The Parthenon sculptures in the British Museum, the Pergamon Altar in Berlin, the Ephesian Parthermonument in Vienna – European museums abound with classical architectural relics referring to places that are distant in both space and time. It is the values inherent in classical heritage that formulate the master narratives of these exhibitions, inscribed in both national and European heritage through the authority of the museum institution. While something as monumental as a reconstruction of a large building in a museum space asserts a strong example of an imagined geography, smaller units, down to single objects, can also define a place that lies far beyond the exhibition. While this place may be not far removed from the museum – as with many objects in the Capitoline Museums in Rome or the Acropolis Museum in Athens – a large body of classical material culture in European museums, especially those north of the *limes* of the Roman Empire, refers to places that are very far removed from the museums – to the cultures surrounding the Mediterranean traditionally identified as the source of European civilisation:

> Across the national museums of Europe, there is an implicit and connective language of material things – objects and architecture – dominated by the motifs of Classical culture. Repeatedly valued and imported by nations across Europe, the ancient cultures of Greece and Rome perform as a trans-European language in defining as different those who live beyond its borders.
>
> (Knell 2011, 22; see also Aronson 2011, 31–34)

The history of the creation of these collections ties into nineteenth- and twentieth-century European colonialism. Classical antiquities were excavated and exported from the countries of origin, both in southern Europe and outside Europe, as an expression of a cultural hegemony enacted mainly by north-west European nation states, driven by an impetus that could be described as a cultural entitlement (Bilsel 2012; Prettejohn 2012; and see chapter 4).

The history of this entitlement brings us to the early Renaissance, when Italian humanists "rediscovered" antiquity – first predominantly understood as Roman. The successful spread of this intellectual paradigm across the learned and courtly milieus of Europe led to the formation of collections of Roman antiquities in Europe in the sixteenth to eighteenth centuries among nobility and the rising class of the bourgeoisie as an expression of cultural refinement and affinity. The displays of these collections focused on the aesthetic qualities of the objects (Jenkins 1992, 58), interpreting them as representations of an objective, trans-historical beauty (Dyson 2006, 142). The collectors were rarely interested in the archaeological context of the objects, the central geographical denominator being that they hailed from Italy.

The humanists' increased engagement with Greek texts from the mid-fifteenth century onwards necessitated a broad distinction in the cultural geography of classical antiquity: that between Greek and Roman culture. This also led to a nascent periodisation, Greece being the cultural predecessor of Rome. It was Johann Joachim Winckelmann who took the defining step in formulating Greece as the predecessor of Roman and therefore European art in his seminal *Geschichte der Kunst des Alterthums* (1764). Winckelmann's ideas of the art of the Greeks as a reflection of their advanced cultural state deeply affected the appreciation of classical art (Jenkins 1992, 60–61; Harloe 2013). Greek art was construed as the basis against which all art from later periods should be measured. Winckelmann's idea of art history as undergoing a progressive development towards beauty before descending into decadence has been seen as the first formulation of four distinct stylistic periods: the Archaic, High, Beautiful and Imitative (following Jenkins 1992, 22, we can conceive of these as equivalents to the Archaic, the Phidian, the Praxitelean and the Roman styles). This periodisation came to have a profound influence on the scholarship of sculpture and subsequently on how classical archaeological material was displayed in the museums of the early nineteenth century and after (Jenkins 1992, 56; Siapkas and Sjögren 2014, 170–171).

From the mid-nineteenth century, the *art historical* approach, with its focus on the nexus between chronology and culture, began to challenge the aesthetic narrative, creating a lasting dichotomy in the potential of interpretation (Dyson 2006, 142; see Jenkins 1992, 56; Siapkas and Sjögren 2014, 90–91 for similar distinctions). The displays presented material in a serialised narrative of civilisations, beginning in Egypt, moving through the Near East, culminating in Greece and ending in Rome (Jenkins 1992, 56) – a systematisation that was realised in the Glyptothek in Munich, for example (Gropplero di Troppenburg 1980, 195–196), and continues to be widely applied in classical collections across Europe. The nexus of geography, chronology and culture was born.

The appropriation of the cultures of antiquity into a narrative of European civilisation, placing ancient Greece as central in this European cultural genealogy, made Greek acquisitions increasingly attractive. Greek material, mainly vases, had been available from southern Italy. Until the foundation of the Greek nation state in 1830 with its restrictive laws on the export of antiquities, collectors and the early European museums had access to the material relics of ancient Greece, as the waning power of the Ottoman Empire gave way to an intensified European cultural hegemony over Greece and Western Turkey (Dyson 2006, 133–134). From the mid-nineteenth century, European and American institutions mounted archaeological expeditions throughout the eastern Mediterranean area in a race to acquire both knowledge and prestigious objects and export them back to their homelands (Prettejohn 2012, 38–104; cf. chapter 4).

The strengthening of the ties between the museum institution and the academic community of classical archaeologists through the late nineteenth and early twentieth centuries meant that the historical and geographical *context* of the material became increasingly important and now began to be emphasised in the displays (Siapkas and Sjögren 2014, 103). The integration of excavation finds into museum collections and the invention of the archaeological site brought into focus a more specific geography of the ancient world. Regional differences within the two large categories of Greek and Roman cultures could now be expressed, simultaneously underscoring the dichotomy between the cultural centres, Athens and Rome, and the peripheries such as the Greek colonies and the Roman provinces. As the imagined geography of classical antiquity took shape, it was not generally placed in a narrative that related it to the culture of the modern nations that now occupied the same area as their ancient antecedents. Even if the nascent Greek nation state was defined by the ideal example of the classical Greeks, this construction was sustained to a large extent not by the Greeks, but by its West European "guarantors" (Tsigakou 1981, 11).

Discourses were established that disenfranchised the modern nations of their ancient heritage because of their lack of civilisation, discourses that continue to echo in discussions of repatriation in twenty-first century Europe, especially in relation to Greece and Turkey (Fouseki 2014, 174–175; Hanink 2017). The imagined geography of the Mediterranean as the cradle of European civilisation was instead connected to the young democracies of Europe, establishing them as the ideological and cultural heirs to classical heritage. As Western European archaeologists excavated and documented the past and moved vast quantities of material culture, housing them in their museums, they created an academic practice to frame the production of knowledge about the classical past. The objects were presented in exhibitions in ways that reflected their scientific value within classical archaeological research paradigms, focusing on establishing typologies most prominently through *Kopienkritik* and *Meisterforschung* (Dyson 2006, 157–162).[2] The aesthetic narrative of the classical display as a frame in which the transcendental aesthetic values of ancient art could be contemplated continued. There was increased focus on the concept of the ancient "masterpiece," understood as a pinnacle of artistic and cultural development, such as the Venus de Milo acquired by the Louvre in 1821 and immediately given a central position in the museum, physically as well as discursively (Dyson 2006, 142; Prettejohn 2006).

New directions in display

Within the last decade, the traditional approaches to exhibiting classical antiquities have been exposed to critical studies, focusing especially on exhibitions of Greek and Roman sculpture. Contemporary exhibitions of classical sculpture still reflect both nineteenth-century aesthetics and twentieth-century art historical narratives of the classical past. Johannes Siapkas and Lena Sjögren argue that this framework results in "a lack of references to the original cultural setting" (Siapkas and Sjögren 2014, 199). In line with this, Elizabeth Marlowe problematises how many Roman sculptures displayed in museums lack an archaeological context (Marlowe 2013, 4). In this line of argument, objects without a cultural (or archaeological) contextualisation are perceived as representative only of the museum context itself and have lost their potential to tell authentic stories of the past. Only by contextualising the sculptures through references to their archaeological contexts so that they represent specific historical points situated in space and time can they tell stories of the cultures of ancient Greece and Rome (Marlowe 2013, 6–7). If the objects have no place outside the museum, they have no place at all.[3] Others have countered this by suggesting that one of the most important focal points of classical reception is the transcendental, inherent aesthetic qualities of the classical sculpture (Beard and Henderson 1995, 51; Vout 2012; Squire 2012, 468–470). Focusing solely on the "original" contexts of classical sculptures disregards the many other contexts they have been part of over time; in the encounter between viewer and object, meaning arises from the aesthetic experience, which may tell us about aspects of the object's meaning in the past (Vout 2012, 446).

This discussion is closely tied to the idea of how authenticity is evoked in the exhibitions. The modern idea of the authentic is central to the display of classical objects, because the fragmentary state of the objects on display underscores their historicity and the temporal distance between then and now (Bilsel 2012, 87). A museum exhibition emphasises the temporal and cultural decontextualisation of the objects, but it strengthens the objects' power to define not merely the museum space but also the place being referred to, the authentic place to which the object belongs. This discussion problematises the role of geographical and cultural reference in establishing the authenticity of the interpretation represented in the exhibition. It also touches upon the critical postcolonial potential inherent in this focus on the role of archaeological context and the academic tradition woven into the production of meaning (Siapkas and Sjögren 2014, 108). This issue has found clearest expression in the ongoing debate over the repatriation of antiquities from north-west European and American museums back to the countries of origin (Gill and Chippindale

2007; Cuno 2012; Fouseki 2014). That debate has affected the Ny Carlsberg Glyptotek, which in 2016 returned a group of illegally acquired artefacts to Italy (Broval 2016; Vuorela and Fals 2016). In reclaiming these archaeological objects, the nations of the Mediterranean define them as part of their heritage and lay claim to the right to interpret them and re-export their new interpretations, challenging the cultural privilege held by northwest Europe since the eighteenth century.

The National Museum: Classical antiquities as heritage-in-between

The nineteenth century marked the birth of the modern museum institution in Denmark. It is in this period that we find the three most significant collections of classical antiquities – Thorvaldsens Museum (opened in 1848), the National Museum (opened in the Prince's Palace in 1849) and the Ny Carlsberg Glyptotek (in which the classical antiquities were put on display in 1906).[4] The central status of classical antiquity as normative heritage in nineteenth-century Denmark was also expressed in the creation of large collections of plaster casts of classical and European sculpture, both in provincial museums, such as the art collection in Aarhus Museum, where the casts were acquired in the 1870s (Bilde 2000), and in the National Gallery, whose cast collection was established in 1895 (Zahle 2005).

As discussed in chapter 1, the National Museum was born out of the Antiquities Commission established in 1807, tasked with establishing a collection of Danish archaeological artefacts and presiding over the preservation of monuments that were seen as essential to a Danish national heritage (Federspiel 2005, 90; Jakobsen 2010, 161). The fundamental changes across Europe, where the shift from feudal anciens régimes based on loyalty to a sovereign monarch and religious affiliation to democracies and enlightened absolutism created a need for institutions that could define the nation in terms of history, culture and people, creating "imagined communities." As discussed in earlier chapters, Denmark had in the early nineteenth century experienced a series of deep crises; the English wars (1801–14), state bankruptcy in 1813 and the loss of Norway in 1814 led to a need for formulation of a new national identity that could provide stability in chaotic times (Federspiel 2005, 92–97; cf. chapter 1).

The concept of heritage as formative for the Dane was expressed clearly in the original mandate of 1807, which states that the Antiquities Commission should define "how the people best could be taught the value of the antiquities that often are dug from the ground." From the start, a state museum was envisioned as an appropriate technology for this task, (Jakobsen 2010, 189). The future director of the National Museum, Christian Jürgensen Thomsen, became secretary of the Commission in 1816 and began the first systematisation of the growing collections, which in 1892 would be renamed the Danish National Museum (Jensen 1992, 49). By then, the museum had been going through a series of mergers of royal collections into a fully formed, albeit small European universal museum. It has retained this format and now holds collections of Danish history from prehistory to the present, ethnographical collections, and a collection of Egyptian, Near Eastern and classical antiquities.

The roots of the National Museum's collection of classical antiquities were the private Kunstkammer of Frederik III (1609–70), founded in 1650, following in the footsteps of European royalty (Jacobaeus 1696, 63). By then, the numbers of classical antiquities were quite limited, but, significantly, they included two marble heads from the Parthenon metopes (Figure 1.2). The Kunstkammer was discontinued in 1825, and the classical antiquities passed first to the Royal Museum of Art. From here, they were incorporated in 1851 into a conglomerate of collections housed at The Prince's Palace, originally built for the later Frederik V in 1743–1744 and given to the Danish state in 1849 (Hein 2001, 166). The first significant addition to the collection of classical antiquities came from Christian VIII (1786–1848), who in 1820 during his grand tour acquired a substantial number of Greek vases that would come form the core of a private, royal collection of classical antiquities. Following the death of Christian VIII, which marked the end of absolutism in Denmark, his collection of Greek vases, passed to the Old Nordic Museum (the name of the collection established by the Antiquities Commission), which already held the classical antiquities from the Royal Museum of Art, under the directorship of Thomsen (Rasmussen *et al.* 2000, 9). This collection of classical antiquities was exhibited for the first time in 1853 as the Antikcabinet in the Prince's Palace. The collection continued to grow through the nineteenth century and was greatly enhanced by finds from the Danish archaeological expeditions of 1902–1914 to the island of Rhodes, and in the 1930s to Hama, Syria (Lund and Rasmussen 1995, 198–200; cf. chapter 4).

Thomsen had travelled widely in Europe, visiting a range of museums with collections of antiquities, including the Louvre, the British Museum and Altes Museum in Berlin (Jensen 1992, 195–208). He considered a collection of classical antiquities to be a natural and necessary part of any European national museum. This is evident from his reaction to the acquisition of the Vasekabinet as expressed in an 1851 letter to historian Lauritz Vedel Simonsen (1780–1858). With the addition of the king's private collection, the National Museum had gone "from having a collection of Classical antiquities one would be ashamed of and which fall through even more by comparison to Thorvaldsen's, to acquiring an expansion which makes it possible to arrange a cabinet of Classical antiquities that will become quite fascinating" (Hermansen 1951, 51). Thomsen realised the drawbacks of being on the periphery of Europe, but he also provided a way to remedy this marginal role and place Denmark at the centre stage: "We cannot compare with the nations that are closer to the source when it comes to precious and beautiful antiquities, therefore we must seek to distinguish ourselves through a better arrangement and a rational display" (Hermansen 1951, 51).

Thomsen was the creator of the archaeological system of periodisation and was appalled at the, to his mind, illogical arrangements of collections according to material that he had encountered in the European museums (Jensen 1992, 357; Hermansen 1951, 51). The classical collections in Thomsen's museum were arranged according to the following periodisation:

1   The Archaic, that which in itself is old or made according to the older taste and style,
2   Art and Antiquity in all its glory and beauty,
3   the waning and the steep decline of art.

(For Danish version see Hermansen 1951, 52)

With this arrangement, which owes much to Winckelmann's theories of the development of classical art, Thomsen wished to create an exhibition that demonstrated visually how the style and art of the ancients were represented across materials to form a coherent cultural development through style (Jensen 1992, 357; Hermansen 1951, 50; Nørskov 2002, 139–140) and to form an exhibition that showed the refinement of the Danish interpretation of classical antiquity, establishing the Danish collection as a frontrunner in terms of academic methodology and theory.

Thomsen's chronological exhibition was short-lived. It was supplanted in 1865 with a new exhibition by his successor Carl Ludvig Müller (1809–1891), who organised it after the principle of materials (Jensen 1992, 358). From the 1930s until refurbishment in 1994, classical antiquities were arranged chronologically but grouped according to material (Lund and Rasmussen 1995, 6). Sophus Müller (1846–1934), director of the National Museum 1892–1921, argued that the inclusion of classical antiquity in the museum showed that Danish culture "is only a small part in the evolution of the whole of Europe and the World" (Müller 1907, 112). Through museum displays that created chronologically comparative narratives, one could come to understand that "also in Classical antiquity there was such an extent of unity in the European culture that the evolution with the barbarians, thus including Denmark, continuously followed in the footsteps of the Classical people" (Müller 1907, 112). Essentially, classical antiquity was seen as the foundation of Danish civilisation (Müller 1907, 119; Antiksamlingen 1950, 3). The application of the chronological narrative was central to the understanding of classical antiquity that the National Museum wished to convey with its display. While classical antiquity was broadly understood as a cultural phenomenon, aesthetics also played a role. Reading the museum guides, we find significant attention being paid to the narrative of the flourishing of the arts in Athens during the classical period (Antiksamlingen 1968, 32), as well as the application of the *Meisterforschung* paradigm in the identification of the painters of Athenian black- and red-figure vases, pointing to the inescapabilty of classical archaeology as art history (Antiksamlingen 1968, 39–44).

The modernity of classical antiquity

The collection of classical antiquities in the National Museum is currently exhibited in a series of rooms on the third floor, shared with the collection of Near Eastern and Egyptian antiquities (Figure 3.1). The collection was moved from the second floor, which it had shared with the Renaissance and ethnographical collections, during extensive refurbishments of the museum between 1988 and 1994. The move initiated the most thorough restructuring of the exhibition since the 1930s (Lund and Rasmussen 1995, 91). The present exhibition at the National Museum is a culture-historical narrative of the Mediterranean cultures from Bronze Age Greece to the fall of the Roman Empire. The exhibition is chronological and is geographically systematised, envisioned by the curators as a "journey around the Mediterranean" (Lund and Rasmussen 1995, 6).

The periodisation follows a schema that has been recognisable since the nineteenth century and is extant throughout classical exhibitions in Europe today. This chronological system is closely associated with geography. Places are related to significant periods in cultural development, and the narrative journeys westwards, from the Near East and Egypt, across Greece, to Rome. The Aegean Bronze Age cultures are followed by early Greek cultures in the Geometric and Archaic periods. Here material from Corinth and Athens – traditionally viewed as the defining places of the Greek Archaic period – are supplemented by material from the Danish Rhodes expedition, showing how Danish archaeologists have contributed to the accumulation of knowledge of these periods and thus making Rhodes a part of the grand narrative of classical archaeology.

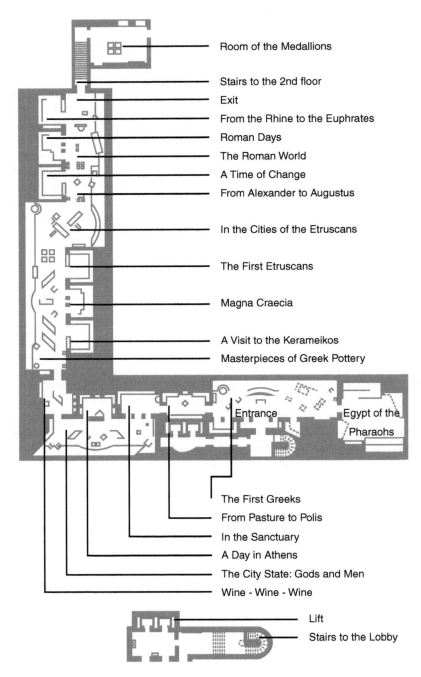

Figure 3.1 Floor plan of the display of the National Museum's collection of classical antiquities

Source: Nationalmuseet

The classical period is represented almost exclusively by Athens, the two fragments from the Parthenon, each in their display case, taking pride of place (Figure 1.2). Magna Graecia, the world of the Greek colonies from the Archaic period to the Roman expansion in the fourth century BC, provides a narrative of the diffusion of Greek culture throughout the Mediterranean, with a geographical focus on southern Italy, conquered by Rome in the third century BC. The westward expansion brought the Greeks into contact with the Etruscans, a culture traditionally represented in museum contexts outside Italy as a link between Greece and Rome. In the exhibition the focus is initially on the cultural exchange between Greek and Etruscan culture. This narrative is punctuated by the cultural landslide let loose by Alexander the Great. The Hellenistic period is communicated as a sweeping overview ("A Time of Change," room 316) of reverberations throughout the ancient Mediterranean, from Athens, across southern Italy, to the absorption of the Etruscan area into the Roman expansion. The centre of the narrative of the early empire is the city of Rome, but the narrative branches off into different geographical settings in the theme "From the Rhine to the Euphrates" (room 318) to illustrate the wide scope and cultural heterogeneity of the Roman Empire (Figure 3.2). The breakdown of this vast empire in Late Antiquity marks the end of the narrative.

Throughout this journey, themes in the exhibition serve to contextualise objects in a narrative that is essentially about the conditions of human life in the past, seeking to "reach beyond the objects themselves back to the people who created and used them" (Lund and Rasmussen 1995, 6). The grand narrative of the exhibition is presented in the first room. Here a section entitled "The Peoples of the Mediterranean" places cultural exchange as a central driver of civilisation, tying the cultures of the Mediterranean together, at the core of the narrative. This is established as an essential precondition of European and, with it, Danish civilisation:

> A world in constant movement and change. New ideas spread like rings in the water. From the Near East to Greece, from Greece to Etruria and Rome. From here northward to France, Germany and Denmark. Many people and many cultures in constant interaction.
>
> (Display text in room 304)

A movement backwards in time and southwards geographically connects Denmark to Europe, and Europe with the cradle of Western civilisation found in the Near East. The presence of the collection of classical antiquities itself in a Danish national museum retroactively confirms this narrative.

The introduction to the exhibition guide presents classical antiquity as "a distant past, yet present as part of the foundation of Denmark today" (Lund and Rasmussen 1995, 6). The discourse is clearer on the museum's thematic website for the Mediterranean/Greece, which explains how Denmark

Figure 3.2 View of the National Museum's room 315, "The Roman World"
Source: Photo by Lærke Maria Andersen Funder 2018

and Europe are connected ideologically and historically to ancient Greece, imbuing its geography with the following values (echoing closely the language of the European Heritage Label in Figure 1.1):

> The seed to many of the concepts that characterise contemporary Europe were sown in Greece in the first millennium BC: words like democracy, politics, philosophy, history and ecology all have Greek roots. . . . Classical Greek culture and art have made a definite mark on Europe's posterity – not at least Denmark, where architects and artists from the seventeenth century and forth were deeply inspired by the Classical ideals. The past lives in the present.[5]

For the visitor walking through the exhibition, Greece is placed as a chronological predecessor to Rome. Roman sculpture, comprising mainly imperial portraits, is described as a result of the reception of Greek art, under the themes "Roman Greece" (room 318) and "The Roman Empire" (room 315). This art historical narrative follows the established trope of the centrality of Greek art in European art history. This narrative is, however, not strongly emphasised in the exhibition. Roman culture is equally represented as a culture of its own – influenced by Greece, Etruria and other Italian peoples, and also in turn affecting them.

The dualistic concept of classical antiquity expressed in the exhibition guide – at once distant yet ever-present – reverberates throughout the exhibition. While engaging with the otherness of the classical cultures when explaining practices such as the Greek *symposion* and the Roman imperial cult, the overall thematic approaches hone in on subjects that are recognisable to the museum visitor, such as the workings of a city and a state in themes such as "From Pasture to Polis" (room 305), politics in "The City State: Gods and Men" (room 307) and religion in "In the Sanctuary" (room 306). The museum objects are contextualised into a narrative which seeks to explain them to the visitor as material manifestations of cultural practices and features that are recognisable to us still. This macro-scale view is matched by the recurrent theme of everyday life, found in both the Greek and Roman exhibitions. Here, the narrative shifts from the focus on broad developments in society to how ancient Greek and Roman citizens lived their lives. Family, childhood, marriage, work life and gender roles are illustrated through the collections, which are exhibited in small rooms that literally make history appear up close and personal for the visitor. While claiming to represent a continuum of cultures that are direct precursors of aspects of European and Danish culture, the exhibition in the National Museum abstains from defining these aspects explicitly. Though a core concept of European identity, democracy is a subtheme of "The City State: Gods and Men," explicit references from the classical past to present-day Denmark and Europe are not drawn apart from the grand narrative of cultural exchange as a precondition for European civilisation at the beginning of the exhibition. This can perhaps be explained as an example of how ingrained the idea of the relevance of the classical heritage is in the National Museum. The significance of the classical heritage as a precursor to European and, with it, Danish identity is an idea of universality in terms of its relation to Western culture. As the root of both Europe and the West, classical antiquity belongs not only in a Danish national museum but in all European national museums.

The narrative presented in the display of the collection of antiquities in the National Museum creates an imagined geography of the classical world where cultural exchange is the driving force in the formation of civilisation and is the core driver behind the complexity and richness of the classical cultures – both on a macro and micro level, between empires and everyday life. The narrative defines the ability to absorb, spread and reform ideas and technology as central not only to Greek and Roman civilisation, but to Europe as a historically and culturally defined place.

Denmark as heir to European tradition

The art historical narrative is, however, present in the exhibition. Several objects are clearly viewed as masterpieces (Lund and Rasmussen 1995, 95) and are visually singled out in the exhibition, placed alone in free-standing glass cases along the main route of the exhibition. The star pieces of the exhibition, the Greek vases from Christian VIII's private collection, are arranged prominently in room 310, "Masterpieces of Greek Pottery," in a narrative that underscores the aesthetic value of the pieces. This is supplemented by a theme on the history of the royal vase collection, applying the historiography of the collection to argue for the place of the collection in the National Museum of Denmark. Thus, the establishment of a collection of classical antiquities in Denmark shows the naturalisation of this particular heritage into Denmark's cultural heritage, which in turn points to a European tradition that Denmark historically has been part of. This logic is also applied in the culture-historical narrative of the exhibition, where the Danish archaeological expedition to Rhodes (rooms 306–307) appears in the exhibition as a metanarrative, integrating the engagement with the classical heritage into Danish heritage (cf. chapter four). The theme "In the Sanctuary" introduces the narrative of the Danish excavation, while subthemes "Visits from the Near East" and "Finds from Cyprus" show how the Danish finds document the central role of the island of Rhodes in the process of cultural exchange owing to "the pivotal position of Rhodes on the sea route between the East and the West" (text in room 306). The Danish excavations focused on the sanctuary of Athena on the Lindian acropolis (cf. chapter four). The importance of this place in the narrative of the exhibition is underscored by a three-dimensional model of a reconstruction of this sanctuary, thus making this a key geographical reference point outside the exhibition.

The classical collection's function as a symbol of Denmark's place in a European cultural tradition of engaging with classical antiquity has also had an effect that, while not visible in the display, is significant in terms of understanding the status of the classical antiquity as Danish cultural heritage. All the exhibited objects from the collections from classical antiquity are designated "of unique national importance."[6] This institutional valuation is the highest classification of heritage value that can be ascribed to an object in a museum collection in Denmark. It defines it as inalienable from Danish cultural identity and therefore to be preserved indefinitely. Selected classical antiquities with this designation are presented on the museum web page as part of a collection of objects that lie at the heart of the National Museum.[7] Among these are a theme on the Hama expedition, where all objects on display are designated as "of unique importance" to Danish heritage not only because they originate in classical antiquity but because they represent Danish engagement with classical antiquity as part of the nation's cultural history.[8] This narrative is also central to the designation of the "Copenhagen Vase," an Attic red-figure amphora, as being of unique national importance: It belonged to Christian VIII and is thus an example of Denmark's participation in the Enlightenment elevation of classical antiquity as European cultural heritage, exemplified through the formation of royal and state collections (Figure 3.3).[9]

Returning to the exhibition, the narrative spun around the National Museum's two fragmentary heads of one of the metopes of the Parthenon shows a strong need to make a connection between Denmark and classical Athens (Figure 1.2). Museums possessing fragments from the Parthenon – such as the Louvre and the Kunsthistorisches Museum in Vienna – never miss a chance to single these out in their exhibitions. In the Danish National Museum, the first thing that confronts the visitor on entering the exhibition is a plaster cast of the metope to which the Danish fragments belong, along with the story of how they were acquired and brought to Denmark in 1687. In the exhibition, only these fragments are treated to a digital version of the otherwise completely analogue display; a short slide show telling the story of the Parthenon and showing how the fragments would have looked in their original context. The symbolic power of the Acropolis in the European cultural narrative is hereby integrated into a Danish national context.

Ny Carlsberg Glyptotek: A modern Maecenas

The Ny Carlsberg Glyptotek opened its doors to the public in 1897 displaying the collection of modern sculpture and art. From 1906, the people of

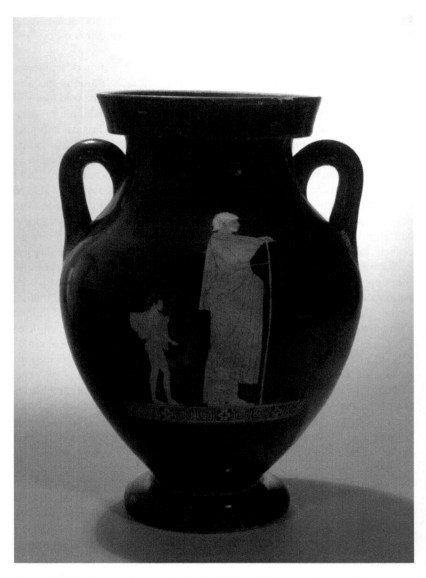

Figure 3.3 The "Copenhagen Vase," The National Museum. Attic red-figure vase, c. 500 BC. Bought for Prince Christian Frederik, the later King Christian VIII, in Paris 1839 by archaeologist and naval officer C. T. Falbe.

Source: Nationalmuseet http://samlinger.natmus.dk/AS/asset/28350

Copenhagen could visit the largest collection of classical art in Northern Europe. The collection was initiated in the late 1870s by Carl Jacobsen. Jacobsen created a considerable collection of classical art and contemporary French and Danish sculpture. Most of the classical collection stem from the late nineteenth-century antiquities market in Rome. Jacobsen was an industrial prince, part of the new network of power developing in a young democracy. Like many of his international counterparts, Jacobsen continued the aristocratic tradition of collecting (Nørskov 2002, 166), but he expanded this practice to match the new democratic ideal by bequeathing his collections to the public. The loss of Schleswig-Holstein in 1864 had dealt yet another blow to a nation still reeling from the catastrophes of the early nineteenth century. Denmark was struggling to find its place in a changed Europe, where the formation of a new kind of citizen was creating a new social and cultural hierarchy, with the bourgeoisie vying to establish themselves as leading citizens through philanthropic endeavours glorifying the nation and helping to shape their fellow citizens to fit the new democratic ideal (Nørregård-Nielsen 2004, 10).

In 1888 Jacobsen and his wife, Otillia (1854–1903), bestowed their collection of modern art and a smaller collection of classical antiquities in a deed of gift to the city of Copenhagen, on the condition that the Danish state and Copenhagen municipality built and paid for a museum fit to house the collection. In 1899 the deed of gift was extended further, by which time the collection now encompassed a considerable number of classical antiquities. Jacobsen intended to create a collection of sculptures, modelled on King Ludwig I's Glyptothek in Munich (Moltesen 2006b, 40). The 1888 deed of gift shows how sculpture, classical as well as modern, was central to Jacobsen's idea of enculturing Denmark in a European context:

> As the Glyptotek holds the most and the best of what the sculptors of our country have created by the impulse of Thorvaldsen, and thus represents an age where our country occupied a distinguished place in the history of European sculpture, especially by the works of Bissen and Jerichau. And since it also holds that which we otherwise miss in this country, a representation of both ancient art and the great creations of the present, we can only wish that it can have its final place in the capital of Denmark, and we will then offer it as a gift for our fatherland.
>
> (Carl and Ottilia Jacobsen's deed of gift, 8 March 1888, published in Jacobsen 1906)

Jacobsen was the first director of Ny Carlsberg Glyptotek and was heavily involved in the architectural design of the museum. He created a European place in Copenhagen. Vilhelm Dahlerup's (1836–1907) historicistic building of 1897 was built to house the collection of Danish and French nineteenth-century sculpture. The entrance echoes Roman triumphal arches, while the façade refers to Venetian Renaissance palatial architecture, drawing lines to the perceived reawakening of European arts (Søndergaard 2006, 21; Østergaard 2011). Hack Kampmann's (1856–1920) building of 1906 is more subdued. Denmark's foremost Art Nouveau architect created a museum that combined both Greek and Roman elements in a neoclassicist style. A red brick façade with evenly spaced double pilasters culminates in a forecourt emulating an ionic ante-temple, completed by a pyramid roof inspired by the Mausoleum of Halicarnassus (Østergaard 2011; Sommer 2009, 281). A bronze copy of Athena Velletri, a Roman sculpture today in the Louvre, crowns the building. The goddess of art, crafts and wisdom oversees the museum and its inhabitants – Jacobsen's collections of classical antiquities (Moltesen 2006a, 28–33).

Kampmann's building also serves the additional purpose of a memorial for Carl and Ottilia Jacobsen (Østergaard 2011, 19–20; Friborg 1998). On the façade of the Kampmann building – actually the back side of the museum – we find a relief by Carl Aarsleff (1852–1918) of the pair in classical guise. Mixing Greek and Roman iconography, Ottilia is styled as the modest Roman or Greek wife, covering her head with a palla or himation, while Carl Jacobsen is shown in a Greek himation, holding a scroll in his right hand, a visual topos adopted from Roman portraiture (Østergaard 2011, 13). The Roman frame of reference is further strengthened by a relief depicting the city of Copenhagen and the Danish state in personified form after the Roman artistic tradition of rendering cities, landmarks, institutions and concepts in human form. Carl Jacobsen is cast here as continuing a tradition of philanthropic patronage stretching back to classical antiquity: as a modern-day Maecenas (Figure 3.4). In the central hall of the Kampmann building, Roman and Greek statues, urns and sarcophagi are set in the colonnade surrounding the central space. The artefacts function both as museum objects and as set pieces of an evocative setting that draws architectural lines to classical Greek sanctuaries (Østergaard 2011, 12) and Roman imperial fora.[10] The room culminates in a temple front raised on a podium, and especially the frieze under the pediment inscribed with the names of Carl and Otillia draw on Roman traditions of donor inscriptions (Figure 3.5). Thus the central agency behind this integration of classical culture into the Danish context is instantiated in the museum's architecture, which abounds in references to both Greece and Rome. Here

Figure 3.4 The Glyptotek as memorial: The Mausoleum façade with a relief by Carl
Aarsleff showing Carl and Ottilia Jacobsen in Graeco-Roman costumes
opposing a relief showing the personifications of Denmark and Copenhagen

Source: Ny Carlsberg Glyptotek, Copenhagen

Figure 3.5 The central hall with porticos and temple front with a memorial inscription for Carl and Ottilia

Source: Photo courtesy of Kim Nilsson. www.glyptoteket.dk/om-museet/arkitekturen/_mg_ 9951-festsalen-ny-carlsberg-glyptotek-foto-kim-nilsson/

Jacobsen created a space that is doubly inscribed in the European classical tradition: The museum space is rendered a place in a discourse that places not only classical antiquity but also its collection and display at the very centre of a European cultural identity. With the Ny Carlsberg Glyptotek, Denmark confirms and materialises this connection. The imagined geographies both of Denmark as European and of Europe as originating from classical antiquity are thus established.

Ny Carlsberg Glyptotek has traditionally understood itself as an art museum (Friborg 2006b, 181; Nielsen and Johansen 1996). Its collections of classical antiquities and modern paintings and sculpture are connected across time and space as works of art (Figure 3.6). The classical antiquities are thus included in the art historical tradition of European museums. This foregrounds classical antiquity for the modern viewer because it is viewed as the very root of the European artistic tradition. This concept of antiquities as art is further underlined by the very strong presence of the founder in much of the museum's presentational programme.

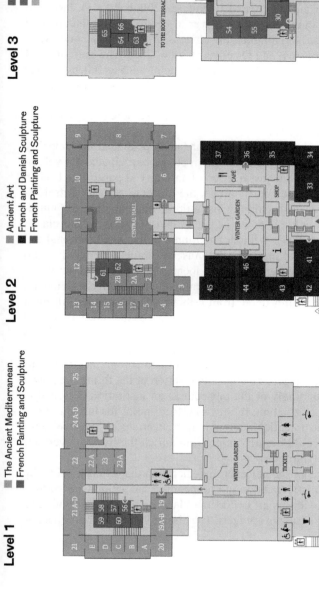

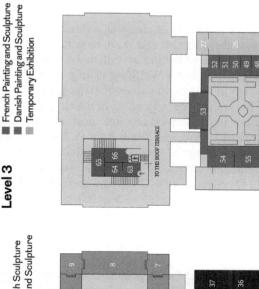

Level 1

■ The Ancient Mediterranean
■ French Painting and Sculpture

Level 2

■ Ancient Art
■ French and Danish Sculpture
■ French Painting and Sculpture

Level 3

■ French Painting and Sculpture
■ Danish Painting and Sculpture
■ Temporary Exhibition

Glyptoteket

Tuesday–Sunday 11–6 pm, Thursday 11–10 pm
Free admission every Tuesday

Figure 3.6 Map of the Ny Carlsberg Glyptotek from 2014 with plans of the displays of the collection of ancient sculpture and of "The Ancient Mediterranean"

Source: Ny Carlsberg Glyptotek

The discourse shows that Jacobsen's concept of classical antiquity as art is fundamental to the identity of the museum and the interpretation of the objects in its collections. The intention behind the collection is made clear in a letter from Jacobsen to his art dealer Wolfgang Helbig in 1887: "With partiality I would take care to collect a number of statues, heads, yes altogether sculpture of the finest sort. The 'speciality' of the Glyptotek should, I believe, be this: to show my fellow citizens the most beautiful things art can create and has created" (Moltesen 2006b, 40–41). Jacobsen was a firm believer in the formative power of beauty: His collection had as its educational goal to enlighten the citizens of the Danish state (Moltesen 2006b, 40; Moltesen and Østergaard 2006, 205). The museum still adheres to this credo, as is evident from statements such as this by former director Flemming Friborg that "the goal is to maintain Glyptoteket as a leading Danish communicator of the arts and lives in the ancient Mediterranean cultures that are the artistic, political and ideological foundation of Europe" (Friborg 2006b, 180).

In the 2000s, faced with the threat that the Copenhagen municipality might cancel its funding, Ny Carlsberg Glyptotek participated actively in the ongoing debate over the justification of antiquity as part of the Danish cultural heritage. In these contributions, the museum presented itself as a "beacon" among Danish cultural institutions, underscoring the museum's authority and cultural potential in its interpretation of the classical heritage (Friborg 2007). Without attention – political, educational and cultural – to this cultural heritage, the museum argued, Denmark could become a cultural backwater in Europe, located at the cultural periphery (Friborg *et al.* 2010). This rhetoric is discursively rooted in the founder's intentions, as shown by this quote from Friborg: "Carl Jacobsen, his most important purpose was to demonstrate for the Danes that our culture had its roots in the Mediterranean" (Pedersen 2007). Classical antiquity is here construed as seminal to both European and Danish cultural identity, and the Ny Carlsberg Glyptotek as bearer and communicator of this important cultural heritage. The conceptualisation of the formative power of art, and correspondingly of the museum as an institution designed to educate the people of a nation, figures as a focal point for the museum's understanding of the potential inherent in its collections: "Carl Jacobsen's conviction that art could beautify, touch and enrich the lives of everyone is still the rule at Glyptoteket."[11]

Another discourse exists, however, together with that of classical antiquity as part of the artistic tradition in Europe: classical antiquity as cultural history. In parallel with his art collections, Jacobsen created a significant collection of mainly Etruscan artefacts. The discourse around this collection was less clear cut. Jacobsen saw the Etruscan collection as an art historical intermezzo between Greece and Rome (Christiansen 2006, 55), necessary in a didactic display of the history of ancient art (Christiansen 2006, 58); yet at the same time, the idea of showing a culture is discernible from the beginning. This dialectic is clearly visible in the successive exhibitions of the collection: After the original Helbig museum of 1891 with its culture-historical narrative and style (Christiansen 2006, 55–57), the collection was refurbished in the 1960s in a more art historical style in an exhibition that was in place until 2006 (Christiansen 2004, 134, 2006, 55; Moltesen and Østergaard 2006, 209–210). The display of the Etruscan collection made in 2006 were viewed as a cultural historical pendant to the collection of ancient art (Friborg 2006b).

Two collections in one museum

The Ny Carlsberg Glyptotek's sculpture collection is displayed in the custom-built galleries in Kampmann's classicistic building.[12] The collection is arranged according to the dominant periodisation, recognisable from museums across Europe and analogous to the exhibition at the National Museum. This conceptualisation lays weight on the trajectory traced by the visitor through the exhibition as a movement through a proxy geography of the Mediterranean, across 1000 years from Greece to Rome. It chronologically and thematically lays the ground for the collection of modern sculpture as part of an art historical narrative of European aesthetics (Friborg 2006a, 13). While Jacobsen initially envisioned his exhibition of sculpture as based purely on aesthetic criteria, already by the end of the 1880s, with the collection still housed in his home, he decided that a chronological exhibition would be the form most conducive to illustrate the history of ancient art (Moltesen 2006a, 30–31). The collection of ancient sculpture in the Kampmann building acts as a counterpart to the collection of modern and contemporary art in the Dahlerup building and to Henning Larsen's (1925–2013) addition to the museum in 1996. The overarching theme connecting the collection of ancient sculpture to the collections of modern art is the influence of the classical works on the arts of modernity and today. The notion of the collection of ancient sculptures as artworks is stressed in the style of display: Presented as unique pieces each resting on individual plinths or hung on walls with plenty of space for each piece, the ancient sculptures are displayed in the same style as the collection of Danish and French modern and contemporary sculpture. Paratexts, such as labels and plates, are discreet and sparse, making the ancient sculptures the absolute centre of attention. The aesthetic quality of the ornate rooms, with monochrome coloured walls and white stucco, and the interplay between them and the sculptures has played a central role in the creation of the exhibition, where the curators focused on how the innate beauty of the sculptures could enhance and be enhanced by the galleries (Moltesen and Østergaard 2006, 209): The display is a *Gesamtkunstwerk*.

Starting in room 6 with Archaic Greece, the exhibition is a chronological narrative of the development of classical sculpture in Europe from the sixth century BC to the fourth century AD. The periodisation on the one hand reflects a shift in geographical focus from Greece to Rome, but on the other keeps referring back to Greece as the wellspring of the classical aesthetic through the theme of *Kopienkritik*. This classical archaeological trope appears across the rooms, expressed through thematic labels such as "Greek sculpture in Roman versions" and in object labels such as that for the marble torso in Figure 3.7: "Herakles. From the environs of Rome. Early 1st century AD . . . This is a copy of one of the works of Polykleitos from around 450 BC." The use of the Greek form of the name asserts the Greek origin of the motif. It is tempting to interpret this approach as a continuation of Jacobsen's formative aesthetics, asserting Greece and Rome as the essentials of European civilisation, connecting the Glyptotek (and by implication Denmark and its people) with this heritage through their place in art history – an idea so thoroughly European that it needs no explicit statement in the exhibition.

The need to move beyond this classical art historical narrative and provide the objects with a cultural context was addressed by the curators in 2006: "During the last 50 years, art history as well as classical archaeology has acknowledged that an isolated presentation of stylistic history . . . is futile in terms of research and dissemination" (Moltesen and Østergaard 2006, 210). They therefore introduced contextualising sociocultural themes in the exhibition, with themes such as "Gods and Heroes: Greek Sculpture in Roman Guise" and "The Greek Art of the Portrait in Roman Service" communicated through texts in the form of plates and text sheets in the display (Moltesen and Østergaard 2006, 211–212). These cultural contextualisations do not stray far from what we may recognise as the modern art historical narrative. However, we also find several settings where the evocative power of the sculptures has been strengthened in order to facilitate an almost interpersonal experience across time and place: The group of portraits from the tomb of the Licinii, Pompey the Great's family burial site in Rome, has been placed at eye level, directly facing the visitor as they enter room 12 (Figure 3.8). While presenting the viewer with some of the most exquisite Roman portraits, this form of display also seeks to thematise family and memory by placing the group of portraits together, reflecting their archaeological context in the tomb. The contextualising

Figure 3.7 Ny Carlsberg Glyptotek, room 8, Roman statue of Hercules
Source: Photo courtesy of Lærke Maria Andersen Funder 2014

Figure 3.8 Ny Carlsberg Glypotek: Collection of sculpture in room 12, displaying the portraits from the Tomb of the Licinii. The star piece, the portrait of Pompey the Great, is placed at the centre of the arrangement

Source: Photo courtesy of Lærke Maria Andersen Funder 2014

approach acknowledges that the classical past as art history may appear distant to the contemporary museum visitor. The museum now attempts to create a framework of familiarity to help the viewer engage with the artworks more easily (Friborg 2006b, 181–182). While insisting on the continued relevance of classical antiquity in the narrative of European art, this relevance is underscored by reference to cultural contexts that make the past present.

Moving one level down, we find "The Ancient Mediterranean," a culture-historical display arranged in a series of rooms in the basement of the Kampmann building. As with the collection of sculpture, these rooms were also built to house the display of the Etruscan collection.[13] The display is based on Jacobsen's Etruscan collection, but it integrates material from the Middle East, Greece, the Greek colonies, and the Roman Empire. The rooms are simple, with white walls and no additional decorations, but the number of objects in mixed media and their arrangement in groupings in display cases make it clear that they are viewed not as unique artworks but as cultural objects to be understood in their relation to other objects and contexts. Explanatory texts are placed by the objects, clarifying their context and use in antiquity.

Walking through the exhibition, we are transported in space and time across 6000 years of history "from the early high cultures in the Middle East to the birth of the Roman Empire." (Christiansen 2008, 2). Thus we move through time and space from beyond Europe into its core. The high cultures of the Middle East, presented in the theme "The Beginning of Everything," introduce the key elements in civilization – religion, technology, state formation and trade – through objects such as religious figurines and fragments of monumental architecture. In the first room (room 19), a map of the Mediterranean region and a film on the myth of the Phoenician princess Europa as the personification of the continent are paired with a theme on coinage and trade, and writing from cuneiform to the alphabet. The myth of Europa being abducted from the Middle Eastern Phoenicia to European Crete by Zeus sets the framework for the narrative of the display: cultural exchange as a precondition for development. This narrative is strengthened in the next theme "A World without Borders" which show how the Phoenicians brought influences from the Middle East and Egypt to Europe, here represented by the Greek and Etruscan cultures. We see here the materialisation of the exhibition's essential idea of the Mediterranean cultures as formed by "the extensive exchange of goods and knowledge, religion and ideologies" (Christiansen 2006, 59). In this narrative, the role of ancient Greece as central in the formation of complex civilisation in the region is stressed in the theme "Society Takes Shape" (room 20), where concepts such as the city state, colonialism, trade and the export of Greek technology and material culture to Etruria are thematised. The Etruscan collection is weaved into this narrative, acting as a materialisation of how the cultural fusion of Greek and Phoenician elements with indigenous Etruscan culture brought about fundamental changes: "Cities arose, huts became palaces and chiefs became princes" (Christiansen 2008, 26). In the progressive chronological narrative, we now follow the development and continuous intercultural interactions of the Etruscan culture until the second century BC, when the Etruscan culture were absorbed into the expanding Roman Empire, "The Etruscans Become Romans" in room 22. Classical Athens is introduced in room 24a, showing how the city reached its zenith in the fourth century BC, noting how "Under these conditions democracy and philosophy, literature and art achieved the forms forever regarded as synonymous with Classical Greece" (Christiansen 2008, 26). In room 24 the theme "Classical: Classicism" shows how European sculpture since Roman times was deeply influenced by classical Greek sculpture, illustrated by an exhibition of two fourth-century Greek grave stelae, a Roman grave monument in classicising style and a plaster cast of a nineteenth-century relief, "The Farewell" (1832) by H. E. Freund (1786–1840). Cultural exchange as a precondition for the Mediterranean civilisations is again thematised through the narrative of Hellenism, showing how Greek culture reached its widest geographical expanse. The conquest of the Hellenistic kingdoms by the Roman Empire during the first century BC entailed yet another cultural exchange, described in a paraphrase of Horace, "The conquerors were themselves conquered – by the imagery of Hellenism." The journeys end in room 25, "Imperial Rome." The idea of belonging to a cultural tradition is shown through the Romans' own uses of past cultures in "The Ancient Civilisations and Rome," while in "The Many Faces of the Romans" portraits from Palmyra, Egypt and Rome show the multicultural nature of the Roman Empire (Figure 3.9).

We could argue that "The Ancient Mediterranean" constructs a cultural mirror image of modern Europe across time, focusing on similarities between present and past lives. Two narrative elements are central in the metadiscourse on the display of the collection, "that the ancient societies basically were driven by the same powers as today: the need for raw materials" (Christiansen 2004, 137) and "that the 'globalisation' of those times around the Mediterranean had consequences that with time reached our latitudes" (Christiansen 2004, 140). This narrative supports the metadiscourse of the museum: that the exhibition should communicate the Mediterranean's "decisive role as a connecting rather than a separating element"

Figure 3.9 Ny Carlsberg Glyptotek, "The Ancient Mediterranean," room 25, under the thematic headline "The Many Faces of the Romans," portraits illustrate the multicultural empire

Source: Photo courtesy of Lærke Maria Andersen Funder 2014

(Christiansen 2004, 138). The interpretation and display of the Etruscan collection is discursively founded in Jacobsen's original idea of the collection as a didactic element in the museum (Christiansen 2004, 134–135, 2006). This approach thus aims to establish classical antiquity as a cultural narrative that can facilitate reflections on ideas of culture and identity in modern Europe (Funder 2014, Supp. 141). That this narrative is still at the centre of the now somewhat reduced display of 2018 is evident from the presentation on the museum web page: "A wealth of finds . . . illustrate in the exhibition how even in the remote past the world was global: and how goods, ideologies, religion and the structure of society throughout the entire Mediterranean world were influenced by intersecting cultural links."[14]

Classicism on display

The current exhibitions in both the National Museum and the Ny Carlsberg Glyptotek ground the classical antiquities in Denmark as part of a European historical narrative of identity and culture. There is nothing particularly Danish about the version of classical antiquity presented, but if we reverse the process we see that Denmark is connected to the classical through its European identity, denoting Denmark as European. The exhibitions function as proxies for the imagined geographies of classical antiquity as they are envisaged in the twenty-first century, but the core of this image goes back to narratives of Europeaness established in the nineteenth century. The presentification of classical antiquity does not question or challenge its importance but continues the discourse of everlasting relevance. The consistency of this narrative is the subject of reflection by the curators of the classical antiquities at the National Museum, understood by them as showing the very core of the importance of the classical heritage and its place in Denmark: "Indeed, there can be no doubt that this heritage is the single most important component of present day Danish culture as expressed by our language, political institutions, art and architecture etc. This realization was at the core of Thomsen's vision . . . And this is why the collections remains an integral part of the Danish National Museum" (Bundgaard and Lund 2002, 175–176). The trope of classical antiquity as paradigmatic for European and Danish culture is thus not questioned, but sustained through a total naturalisation. The relevance of classical antiquity is furthermore bound up with the idea of classical antiquity's potential to provide a place for reflection on, and even critique of, our own culture, an argument we can recognise from the discussions on the relevance of *Oldtidskundskab* in Danish upper secondary schools (cf. chapter 3). While this narrative features in the metadiscourse especially by the Ny Carlsberg Glyptotek, it is not prominent in the displays. Of the three displays, this narrative is most clearly formulated in the display "The Ancient Mediterranean" in the Ny Carlsberg Glyptotek, where the introductory display framing Europe as both a place and myth of civilisation invites the museum guest to read themselves into the complex story of European culture. The idea of classical antiquity as part of *Bildung* and the roles of the museums as institutions of *Bildung* becomes evident as subtexts to both narratives. The museum displays provide the visitors with knowledge of classical antiquity and through this, knowledge of themselves as part of a larger European culture.

The lack of meta-communication and direct reflection on the role as cultural paradigm ascribed to classical antiquity – on how and why classical antiquity is made relevant – in the display reflects the degree to which this narrative is naturalized, indeed almost self-evident. The homogeneity of both the culture historical and art historical narratives between the two institutions indicate that classical antiquity has attained a monolithic character as part of the grand narrative of Danish cultural identity. In this narrative, the imagined geography of Classical antiquity remains a commonplace, rather than unfolding as a source of reflection and critique.

Notes

1 This chapter does not provide an analysis of the full chronological development of exhibitions of classical antiquities in the National Museum or Ny Carlsberg Glyptotek. For historical overviews on the two institutions see Moltesen (2012); Friborg and Nielsen (2006); Nørskov (2002); Jensen (1992); Rasmussen *et al.* (2000). The exhibitions that serve as case studies were mounted within a time span of fifteen years: The exhibition at the National Museum was mounted in 1994, while the two exhibitions at Ny Carlsberg Glyptotek were in 2006.

2 *Kopienkritik* is a research paradigm aimed at reconstructing Greek original sculptures through the meticulous study of later, often Roman, copies. As a positivistic endeavour, *Kopienkritik* was founded on the assumption that the original piece could be deducted from typological analysis of the development of motives and style in sculpture, relying on this technique to peel away the layers of appropriation until the naked original form appeared (Fürtwangler 1893). *Meisterforschung* seeks to attribute sculpture to individual ancient artists through a rigorous study of style and technique. A similar attitude to Attic vases was most famously practised and developed by John Beazley (1885–1970).

3 This critique has coincided with a turn towards a historical and contextual interpretation of the material in museums of classical antiquities, seeking to place the developments in ancient art within a social framework. Examples include the 2013 redesign of the Ashmolean classical collection, the Capitoline Museums' exhibitions of sculpture from Roman gardens and the Louvre's exhibition on Roman Africa (Pasquier *et al.* 1997, 34; Martinez 2011, 37; Walker 2013, 408).

4 Thorvaldsens Museum is devoted to the works of Danish sculptor Bertel Thorvaldsen (1770–1844). It is essentially a biographical museum, so Thorvaldsen's personal collection of classical antiquities (Melander 1993) along with the collections of archivalia and personalia serve to illuminate him and his time more than to represent a continuous engagement with classical antiquity in Denmark.

Since its collection of classical antiquities remains as first set up in 1848, it cannot give any indication of changing paradigms in the reception of antiquity in Denmark through exhibition analysis. However, as Denmark's first public museum building, Thorvaldsens Museum stands as a monument to the central role of classicism in the formation of the citizen in nineteenth-century Denmark: from its classicising architecture by Michael Gottlieb Bindesbøll (1800–1856) to the initiative by the city of Copenhagen to finance a museum for Thorvaldsen's oeuvre and private collection.

5 Middelhavslandene/Grækenland; https://natmus.dk/historisk-viden/verden/middelhavslandene/graekenland/ (last visited 16 April 2018).

6 "Enestående National Betydning": see Kulturministeriet (2003). This designation is part of a scale of value that all Danish museums were asked to use to evaluate their collections by the Ministry of Culture in 2003 in order to identify which objects should receive prioritised conservation and care, and – at the other end of the scale – which objects hold so little significance that they can be discarded.

7 The National Museum, Genstande af enestående betydning; https://natmus.dk/historisk-viden/temaer/genstande-af-enestaaende-betydning/ (last visited 1 May 2018).

8 The National Museum, Fræk Abekat; https://natmus.dk/historisk-viden/temaer/genstande-af-enestaaende-betydning/genstande-fra-antiksamlingen/fraekabekat/ (last visited 1 May 2018).

9 The National Museum, Københavnervasen; https://natmus.dk/historisk-viden/temaer/genstande-af-enestaaende-betydning/genstande-fra-antiksamlingen/koebenhavnervasen/ (last visited 1 May 2018).

10 The temple façade, incorporating both Greek and Roman references, can also be interpreted as referring back to classical architecture more freely. The central hall contains features that can be attributed to Roman architecture: the peristyle surrounding a central courtyard with a Roman mosaic inlaid in the floor harks back to the Roman impluvium, a central architectural feature in villas (Sommer 2009, 279), and the donor inscription on the architrave is a Roman rather than Greek feature.

11 Ny Carlsberg Glyptotek, "What is Glyptoteket?" www.glyptoteket.com/about-the-museum/what-is-glyptoteket/ (last visited 5 April 2018).

12 The analyses are based on material collected in 2010 and 2014. The display of the collection of ancient sculpture has not been restructured significantly. "The Ancient Mediterranean" has undergone substantial changes and been reduced in 2016–2017. Therefore, some of the displays referred to are no longer exhibited.

13 Since parts of the display have been reduced, some of the texts referred to in this analysis are no longer on display. We therefore refer directly to the companion to the exhibition by Christiansen 2008.

14 Ny Carlsberg Glyptotek, "The ancient Mediterranean." www.glyptoteket.com/udstilling/the-ancient-mediterranean/ (accessed 14 June 2018).

4 Excavating a wonder of the ancient world

Danish classicism in the field

Starting out from the basic question of where Danish classical archaeologists have been active in the field, this chapter digs deeper into the discourses of heritage and identity that underpin their fieldwork in the Mediterranean. Specifically it investigates the history of Danish archaeological fieldwork in Bodrum, Turkey (ancient Halikarnassos), which began in 1966 and which has continued until very recently.[1] This fieldwork is closely tied to and a direct outcome of a particular kind of academic classicism that has motivated European scholars for centuries to search out material remains of great civilisations outside of their home countries, attesting to a variety of imagined geographies in the process.

The chief protagonist of this chapter is Kristian Jeppesen (1924–2014), whose scholarship, in spite of its singular direction, is characteristic of Danish academic classicism as practised in the twentieth century. Jeppesen's work in Bodrum focused on the Mausoleum, a monumental funerary complex constructed in the mid-fourth century BC for the burial of the Karian satrap Maussollos and his sister-wife Artemisia II in the heart of the ancient city. From the Hellenistic period onwards, the Mausoleum was included in the lists of world wonders compiled by Greek and Roman authors, giving birth to a concept with a remarkable longevity and resonance right up until the present day. Even in antiquity, the design of the Mausoleum provided a model for other monuments, such as the second-century-BC Lion Tomb at Knidos and the first-century-BC Mausoleum of Augustus in Rome. Much later, key features of the Mausoleum, notably its stepped pyramid roof, served as reference points in twentieth-century architectural classicism around the world.[2] For example, well before Jeppesen's excavations began, architectural references to the Mausoleum had proliferated in Denmark. As we saw in the previous chapter, the stepped pyramid of Kampmann's 1906 expansion of the Ny Carlsberg Glyptotek was inspired by contemporary reconstructions of the Mausoleum (Figure 3.4; and see Østergaard 2011, 10–20). Not long after, the National Exhibition in 1909 in Aarhus included a building presented by the Danish Post and Telegraph and adorned with a

Figure 4.1 Postcard from the 1909 National Exhibition (*Landsudstillingen*) in Aarhus, showing classically inspired architecture, including a Mausoleum-like pyramidal roof

pyramidal roof that again referenced the Mausoleum (Figure 4.1; Bender 2008).[3] The act of excavating the Mausoleum thus already held considerable symbolic capital, both internationally and in the Danish context. Although they were rarely made explicit in Jeppesen's work, the discourses of classicism traced in preceding chapters are instrumental in legitimating the fieldwork as well as the form of its presentation to Danish audiences. This chapter will begin by discussing the history of classical field archaeology in the Mediterranean, in order to investigate the particularities of the Danish work in Bodrum. The following two sections will focus on Jeppesen's efforts to excavate and to reconstruct the Mausoleum, focusing especially on how his academic training produced very particular forms of classical heritage. Finally, we turn to the issue of how the archaeology of Bodrum has been approached by Danish archaeologists in more recent work, as well as some of the challenges that currently face Mediterranean field archaeology more generally in light of the changing relationship between Europe and Turkey.

Classicism in the field

The practice of sending archaeologists to foreign countries has a long and chequered history, which scholars in recent years have linked to naive realism and cultural imperialism in both its formal and informal guises (Díaz-Andreu 2007, 99–130; Siapkas 2017, 130–132). Most accounts of the origins of the discipline have indeed tended to neglect the contribution of what Benjamin Anderson has called "local interpreters," that is, the "people for whom a given object formed part of everyday experience" (Anderson 2015, 452). Recent work on the historiography of classical archaeological practice has thus shed an increasingly critical light on the legacy of Euro-American work in Mediterranean countries. Margarita Díaz-Andreu, for instance, points to the close ties between nineteenth-century archaeological practices and deep-rooted contemporary ideologies such as nationalism and colonialism (Díaz-Andreu 2007; see also Shanks 1996; Kohl *et al.* 2007). Furthermore, in his work on the history of the American School of Classical Studies at Athens, Jack Davis pinpoints the academic habitus that profoundly shaped that institution's history during its formative years (Davis 2003, 148). Davis argues for the need to unsettle the epistemological security that continues to underpin agendas and approaches within the discipline, such as the tendency to focus predominantly on monumental architecture dating to the classical period. This selective approach to classical field archaeology is also strikingly evident in Jeppesen's work at Bodrum, as we shall see.

The development of the discipline of classical archaeology over the course of the nineteenth century underlined its increasing role as an arena for competition for political prestige among European nations, not least through the acquisition of monumental antiquities sourced in the Near East and the Mediterranean (Jenkins 1992; Prettejohn 2012, 38–103). From the middle of the century, north-west European nations founded archaeological institutes (or "schools"), primarily in Rome and Athens.[4] Fuelled by the practices of classicism in contemporary society, large-scale excavations undertaken by European nations starting in the mid-to-late nineteenth century increased the intensity and ambition of archaeological fieldwork in the Mediterranean. Foreign schools and museums sponsored sustained fieldwork campaigns, often competing against each other in order to secure the most prestigious sites in intensive negotiations with local governments and landowners (Marchand 1996, 75–115; Dyson 2006, 86–132). This new era began in 1875, when the newly unified German state opened excavations at Olympia, site of the ancient Olympic Games. In 1892, the French school that was already active on Delos launched excavations at Delphi. The Americans soon followed, beginning work at Corinth in 1896. Excavations often required the demolition of entire villages, as well as the routine clearance of post-classical layers without any form of documentation. Many of the objects uncovered – even whole buildings – were transferred to museums in the countries that had sponsored excavations, in the face of local opposition from both populations and politicians (Hamilakis 2013). Yet these large-scale and long-running excavations remain an important legacy of the discipline. German, French and American archaeologists are thus still active at Olympia, Delphi and Corinth, respectively. They have furthermore defined more generally how archaeological knowledge in the Mediterranean is produced and presented, effectively constituting a particular form of academic colonialism.

Danish archaeologists were present in the Mediterranean from early in the nineteenth century, through the activities of prominent travellers and scholars (Rathje and Lund 1991; Christiansen 2000, 18–33). These included the philologist Peter Oluf Brøndsted, who participated in several excavations in Greece between 1806 and 1811 (Rasmussen *et al.* 2008), as well as the naval officer Christian Tuxen Falbe (1792–1849), who conducted excavations in the 1830s at Carthage, whence a number of finds are now in the National Museum in Copenhagen (Liventhal 1986). These initiatives followed in the footsteps of Danish scientific expeditions in the Mediterranean and Near East that constituted major nation-building investments sponsored by the king. These included the Royal Danish Arabia Expedition (1761–1764), whose only returning member, Carsten Niebuhr, reached as far as Yemen and India, collecting and describing a wide range of materials along the way and even bringing a large number of objects home to the Royal Kunstkammer (Sortkær 2008; Hansen 2016).

At this time, Danish classical archaeology was closely tied to the National Museum, although a university chair had also been established (Johansen 1943; Riis 1979).[5] The chair was often held jointly between classical philology and archaeology, as in the case of Brøndsted (cf. chapter 2). In 1859, Johannes Ludovicus Ussing (1820–1905) was appointed to this chair at the University of Copenhagen (Ussing 1906, 101, 105–106). He had previously defended a dissertation in Latin on the ancient names of Greek vases in 1844 (Ussing 1844). Although Ussing never excavated himself, he travelled extensively in Greece, Asia Minor, and Egypt, and he published widely on his archaeological journeys (Ussing 1873, 1882). As member of the board of the Carlsberg Foundation from 1887 to 1902, he was instrumental in paving the way for Danish excavations in the Mediterranean, academically as well as financially (Ussing 1906, 227–228). Apart from being the patron of the Ny Carlsberg Glyptotek, the Carlsberg Foundation had previously sponsored expeditions to Greenland (Glamann 1976, 128–129), and Ussing actively promoted his ambition that Danish archaeologists should begin excavations of their own in the Mediterranean. In his posthumously published memoirs, Ussing notes how the new era of large-scale excavations in the second half of the nineteenth century had carved out a new role and importance for archaeology, urging Danish scholars to follow the examples of their European (and American) colleagues:

> It is no wonder that everyone who loved classical antiquity and was waiting to see it present itself in its true form was eager to participate in the momentous clear-up. Germany's example was followed by other great nations. France, England, North America, Russia and Italy spent considerable amounts on it. But should not also the smaller states, whose interest and eagerness were no less than the others, should they not also be able to contribute to this common work in the service of culture? And was Denmark not particularly beckoned there, the land which not only by its investigations into the Nordic and prehistoric archaeological field occupies a leading position in this science, but also within classical archaeology both through scientific works and with its rich museums, has acquired the claim to inhabit the inner circle?
>
> (Ussing 1906, 227–228)

Ussing here directly evokes the imagined geography of classicism, in which Denmark's place is secured by two elements: first, by the material heritage of its rich collections of classical antiquities, whose importance was self-evidently displayed as a claim to Danish ownership of classical heritage and thus membership of the "club" of European nations that undertook their own excavations in the Mediterranean; and second, by the contributions of Danish academia to the discipline of archaeology, going back to the efforts of Jürgensen Thomsen and Worsaae (see chapter 3). Ussing describes these scholarly achievements as giving Denmark access to the "inner circle" of nations that work in the service of European culture.

Ussing played a fundamental role in the development of Danish field projects in the Mediterranean by securing the economic support of the Carlsberg Foundation (see chapter 1). The search for a suitable site then began. Changes in Greek legislation made it increasingly difficult to export any antiquities that were found, and sites such as Kleonai and Nemea on the Greek mainland were thus dismissed, as was Cyrene in modern Libya (Ussing 1906, 228). However, the archaeological potential of western Asia Minor was becoming increasingly apparent through the German and Austrian excavations at Ephesus, Priene and Pergamon (the latter being the topic of Ussing 1897). Eventually, the choice of site for the first major Danish excavation in the Mediterranean fell upon the acropolis of Lindos on the island of Rhodes, then part of the Ottoman Empire. The main campaigns were carried out between 1902 and 1905, although work continued at a smaller scale until the outbreak of the First World War. Excavations were led by Karl Frederik Kinch and Christian Blinkenberg, then curator at the National Museum (Ussing 1906, 228–229; Blinkenberg 1941; Dyggve 1960; Dietz and Trolle 1974, 9–16). The contribution of the Carlsberg Foundation amounted to the large sum of 60,000 Danish kroner (equivalent to 4.15 million DKr at 2017 rates), beginning a tradition of funding Danish field archaeology in the Mediterranean. The excavations on the Lindian acropolis followed nineteenth-century practices, with the removal of vast amounts of earth and large-scale demolition of post-classical houses and buildings. Many of the important finds from the excavations were sent to the Danish National Museum, where they still constitute an important component in the classical exhibitions (see chapter 3). Through archaeological excavation and with the help of a private foundation, Denmark had thus acquired another rich hoard of antiquities that consolidated its place as a European nation rooted in classical heritage.

The work at Lindos was followed by excavations in Kalydon, Greece (1926–1935), and Hama, Syria (1931–1938). Figure 4.2 shows the location of these and other Danish fieldwork projects in the countries around the Mediterranean. Viewed through this geographical lens, Danish classicism in the field has two main centres. The first centre is the eastern Mediterranean, with particular emphasis on Greece, Syria and, to a lesser extent, Turkey and Cyprus.[6] This demonstrates just how much classical field archaeology owes not only to Hellenism but also to the long tradition of European "expeditions" to the Near East and beyond, as with the Danish example of Niebuhr's eighteenth-century travels. Although Denmark was never a colonial power in the Mediterranean, its scholarly endeavours were indeed repeatedly tied to various degrees of informal colonialism. The second centre is Italy, with particular emphasis on Rome and its immediate vicinity, often focusing on imperial monuments and constituting a counterpoint to the Hellenic outlook of many other field projects. It is also worth noting some of the gaps. Beyond Tunisia, there is, for example, a notable absence of any work in the western Mediterranean. The choice of sites to excavate primarily reflects the interests of individual Danish archaeologists, but it is also revelatory of how archaeology is believed to be able to contribute to a sense of Danish and European identity construction. Hellenism is a strong component in the emphasis of excavation of sites that have yielded Greek material culture, a trend that is also clear on the broader Euro-American scale (Davis 2003, 163). Indeed, in the formal and informal communication relating to the planning and execution of classical field projects, one repeatedly encounters the tropes of classicism identified in chapter 2.

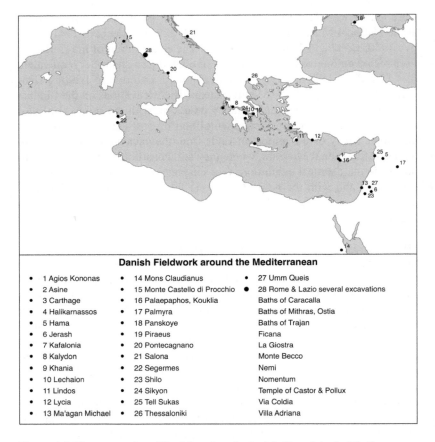

Danish Fieldwork around the Mediterranean

• 1 Agios Kononas	• 14 Mons Claudianus	• 27 Umm Queis
• 2 Asine	• 15 Monte Castello di Procchio	● 28 Rome & Lazio several excavations
• 3 Carthage	• 16 Palaepaphos, Kouklia	Baths of Caracalla
• 4 Halikarnassos	• 17 Palmyra	Baths of Mithras, Ostia
• 5 Hama	• 18 Panskoye	Baths of Trajan
• 6 Jerash	• 19 Piraeus	Ficana
• 7 Kafalonia	• 20 Pontecagnano	La Giostra
• 8 Kalydon	• 21 Salona	Monte Becco
• 9 Khania	• 22 Segermes	Nemi
• 10 Lechaion	• 23 Shilo	Nomentum
• 11 Lindos	• 24 Sikyon	Temple of Castor & Pollux
• 12 Lycia	• 25 Tell Sukas	Via Coldia
• 13 Ma'agan Michael	• 26 Thessaloniki	Villa Adriana

Figure 4.2 The geography of Danish archaeological fieldwork in the Mediterranean
Source: Niels Bargfeldt, based on Rathje and Lund 1991, 38, Figure 14

Excavating the wonder

We turn now to Bodrum, to explore the links between classicism and archaeological practice in more detail. The primary attraction for Danish archaeologists in coming to Bodrum was the considerable scholarly prestige attached to the reconstruction of the Mausoleum, but the Danes were far from the first to explore this wonder of the ancient world. Even before the age of modern archaeology, numerous scholars and explorers had sought to reconstruct the original appearance of the Mausoleum (*Maussolleion* 2, 119–214). The Mausoleum is described by several ancient authors, most importantly Pliny and Vitruvius, who give us the names of famous classical Greek sculptors and architects involved in its construction, as well as crucial information about the layout and dimensions of the monument and its place within the city (*Maussolleion* 2, 13–101; Jenkins and Waywell 1997). These texts remain fundamental to our understanding of the Mausoleum, and a whole volume of the excavation series initiated by Jeppesen is dedicated to squeezing every little technical detail out of them (*Maussolleion* 2). On this basis, the Mausoleum is reconstructed as a quadrangular structure some 45 m tall, with a pyramidal roof, and adorned with a rich assortment of statues and sculpted friezes. The Mausoleum itself was situated on an enormous 25,000 m² terrace that constituted the key component in the larger city plan laid out by Maussollos when he moved the Karian capital from Mylasa (modern Milas) to Halikarnassos (*Maussolleion* 3). It is not known when or how the Mausoleum fell into disrepair, but the region's frequent earthquakes may have been a contributing factor. Generally, Halikarnassos's history during the first millennium AD is poorly known and has been the subject of limited research (Poulsen 2011). However, the demolition of the Mausoleum in the fifteenth and sixteenth centuries is well documented. At this time, architectural blocks and sculptures from the Mausoleum site were removed by the Hospitaller Knights to the Zephyrion peninsula for the construction of the castle of St Peter, the most dominant monument in the city even today.

Eyeing the prize of excavating a wonder of the ancient world, early archaeological exploration in Bodrum followed the pattern of colonial-style classical archaeology described above. In 1852, Charles Newton had left his curatorial position at the British Museum to become vice-consul on Lesbos, which placed him close to the considerable archaeological treasures on the Aegean coast (Jenkins 1992, 171–183; Cook 1997). The diminishing power of the Ottoman sultan increasingly allowed European scholars to carry out extensive archaeological exploration and to transport their finds back to their home countries. Newton arrived in Bodrum in November 1856 on the British warship *Gorgon* with a crew of 150 men (Newton 1862, 86). His excavations at the site of the Mausoleum began two months later. At this time, Bodrum was a small fishing village with a mixed population of Muslims and Christians. In 1857, Newton unearthed a rich cache of sculptures, including colossal statues commonly identified as Maussollos and Artemisia, as well as the so-called Amazon frieze, which were shipped back to London. Today it is in the galleries of the British Museum that one comes face to face with most of the sculptures that originally adorned the Mausoleum (Jenkins 1992, 97–99). Newton's export of the Mausoleum's sculptures led to clashes with the Ottoman authorities, who consequently strengthened their antiquities laws in order to deter Europeans from transporting them out of the country (Díaz-Andreu 2007, 112–113). Attempts to reconstruct the Mausoleum from this point onwards were based on the results of Newton's excavations as well as the subsequent investigations by Alfred Biliotti in 1865, which aimed to locate further sculptural finds for the British Museum (*Maussolleion* 3.1, 117–173).

Almost 100 years after Newton's expedition to Bodrum, Jeppesen turned his attention to the Mausoleum. Jeppesen first trained as an architect at the Royal Danish Academy of Fine Arts, being awarded a diploma in architecture in 1949, and then he obtained a degree in classical archaeology from the University of Copenhagen in 1952. This interdisciplinary profile is sometimes referred to as archaeological *Bauforschung* (historical architectural research), which, as the name indicates, is a discipline with a particularly strong research tradition in Germany (Gruben 2000). *Bauforschung* is a technical and empirical discipline that combines the precise recording of architectural remains with a deep practical knowledge of how Greek and Roman architects worked. Jeppesen's first introduction to Turkish archaeology came through participation in 1950–1951 in the Swedish excavations at the important Karian sanctuary of Zeus at Labraunda, some 60 km inland from Bodrum (Jeppesen 1999, 39, 2011). In 1958, Jeppesen was appointed to the professorship of classical archaeology at Aarhus University, where he was responsible for the development of a small study collection which, under his curatorial oversight, developed into the Museum of Ancient Art and Archaeology, containing plaster casts of classical sculptures and a small collection of antiquities, mostly pottery and coins (Guldager 1993; Bilde 2000). The exhibits that he curated for the museum were rooted in his own research interests, focusing in particular on the Parthenon, one of the most important monuments of European classicism, and later the Mausoleum of Halikarnassos.

Also in 1958, Jeppesen defended his higher doctoral dissertation or *Habilitation*, a study of three major monuments in mid-fourth-century BC architecture with the Mausoleum as his first case (Jeppesen 1958). His normative comments on the selection of case studies go the very core of classicism, which is also expressed in the dissertation's title, *Paradeigmata*:

> Deliberately I have concentrated on items of *primary* importance in the history of architecture, presenting problems too complicated to be dealt with in terms of an encyclopedia, and such, particularly, for the reconstruction and interpretation of which a fresh study of the sources might prove especially rewarding.
>
> (Jeppesen 1958, xvii, emphasis added)

After scrutinising the primary sources and reviewing the multitude of Mausoleum reconstructions put forward across several centuries, Jeppesen concluded that more work carried out with modern excavation methods would be required to advance the issue further. Yet this did not restrain him from proposing a series of new reconstruction drawings of the Mausoleum in the dissertation (Figure 4.3; Jeppesen 1958, 61–64, figures 48–51). This early reconstruction looks radically different to those that he proposed after his excavations in Bodrum (see below). In the dissertation's other two case studies, on the Arsenal of Philo in the Piraeus and the Ionic Portico at Eleusis, he followed a similar approach, closely studying the textual and archaeological evidence and then proposing new reconstructions by way of conclusion.

In noting that Newton had "left a considerable part of the immediate surroundings of the site wholly untouched or just partially explored," the text of Jeppesen's dissertation foreshadowed his later work at the Mausoleum (Jeppesen 1958, 152). Beginning in 1963, he thus repeatedly visited Bodrum, where he investigated architectural fragments from the Mausoleum that had been reused in various parts of the Castle of St Peter, often with the sculptural decoration hidden inside its walls. Through this meticulous work, which required great attention to small details and the well-trained eye of an architectural connoisseur, he discovered further fragments of the Amazon frieze (*Maussolleion* 1, 9–10). These finds once again suggested to him that further aspects of the many mysteries of the Mausoleum could be illuminated if new excavations were carried out at the site.

On 13 April 1966, with the support of the Carlsberg Foundation, Jeppesen thus began excavations at the site of the Mausoleum, although first on a very limited scale. The social and political context was very different in Turkey in the 1960s than it had been in the time of Newton or of the Danish work at Lindos at the beginning of the century. In the wake of the First World War and the subsequent War of Independence, the Ottoman Empire had been transformed into the Turkish Republic under the leadership of Mustafa Kemal Atatürk (1881–1938). A process of modernisation and Westernisation had been implemented, including the translation of classical Greek authors into Turkish (Williams 2013, 123). Similarly, taking inspiration from Europe, Turkish archaeology became subsumed and developed within this new nationalist project (Özdoğan 1998; Bonini Baraldi et al. 2013). The export of antiquities uncovered by foreign excavations was no longer possible. Bodrum had been transformed as well (Mansur 1972). At the beginning of the twentieth century, its Greek population was exchanged with Muslims from Crete (Mansur 1972, 10–11). Due to its isolated location, Bodrum was frequently put to use by the authorities as a place to which political dissidents were exiled. In 1925, the author Cevat Şakir Kabaağaçlı (1886–1973) arrived as a prisoner and fell in love with the town, beginning a life-long engagement with its people and history. Using the pen name

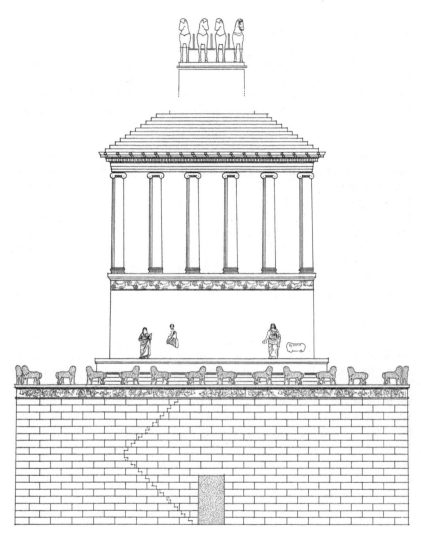

Figure 4.3 Jeppesen's 1958 reconstruction of the Mausoleum

Source: After Jeppesen 1958, 63

of the Fisherman of Halikarnassos (*Halikarnas Balıkçısı*), Şakir helped to revive local and national interest in archaeology as well as in the role of ancient authors, notably Homer. In his writings and radio shows, he criticised the Western focus on Athens and the contributions of Greece, whereas he believed the contribution of Anatolian culture to have been overlooked (Williams 2013, 126). He also played a key role in attracting new visitors to Bodrum, which increasingly developed into a flourishing resort town. From the late 1960s onwards, foreign tourists began to visit, paving the way for the town's development into one of the most popular resorts in the Mediterranean and the large-scale construction of hotels, bars and restaurants (Mansur 1999). The rapid expansion of the town and other parts of the peninsula has in turn necessitated a string of rescue excavations over the years. Finds from these excavations, in addition to the unique and important shipwrecks excavated by the US-based Institute of Nautical Archaeology, populate the Museum of Underwater Archaeology, which opened officially in 1964 and is housed in the castle (Alpözen 1983).[7]

Jeppesen's initial excavations focused on areas not investigated by Newton, tracing the walls that supported the massive terrace on which the Mausoleum was situated. However, in 1970, it became possible to re-excavate the site of the Mausoleum in its entirety (*Maussolleion* 1, 13). This operation was made possible, in Jeppesen's own words, through the acquisition of the Mausoleum plot "for a cheap buck and a bottle of whisky" (Jeppesen 1999, 46). The large quantities of earth that were uncovered in this campaign were used for the construction of Bodrum's new marina. As part of this large-scale work over the following years, the Mausoleum tomb chamber was exposed (*Maussolleion* 4). The Mausoleum was excavated down to its foundation, and a series of pre-Maussollan structures were identified underneath (*Maussolleion* 6). An undisturbed sacrificial deposit with the remains of five oxen, twenty-five sheep or goats, eight lambs, three roosters, ten hens and eight pigeons was excavated on the staircase leading to the tomb chamber, constituting one of the most significant scientific outcomes of Jeppesen's work (*Maussolleion* 1, 21–110). The eighth and final field season at the Mausoleum concluded on 31 July 1977. Over the course of 11 years, the Danish excavations had uncovered thousands of architectural fragments and a large number of small finds.

After the completion of the excavations and right up until a few years before his death in 2014, Jeppesen returned to Bodrum year after year in order to study the fragments in pursuit of a new and more precise reconstruction of the Mausoleum. The post-excavation phase of the project continued for more than 20 years, and the final of seven volumes publishing its main results appeared only in 2004 (*Maussolleion* 6). In his publications of the Mausoleum, Jeppesen never explicitly addressed how this work contributed to our understanding of the ancient world at large. Its importance was largely self-explanatory, following a logic closely tied to the tropes of classicism and the reasoning that he followed in the selection of case studies for his dissertation. Jeppesen's work on the Mausoleum thus emphasised the importance of "a wonder of the classical world" whose architectural reconstruction had been fiercely debated for centuries and which now finally had come up for robust revision on the basis of modern archaeological excavations (*Maussolleion* 1, 9–10). The European fascination with the building across several centuries was what made his studies worthwhile. Jeppesen's approach to the Mausoleum and classical heritage more generally was rooted in the discourses of Hellenism that had emerged in nineteenth-century Europe and that informed his aesthetic sensibilities. This is evident from his choice of monuments to work with, as he sought out historically significant and unique examples of classical architecture. His approach was technical and down-to-earth, true to the traditions of archaeological *Bauforschung*. Jeppesen indeed stayed true to the ideals of classicism throughout his career. For example, he wrote a book on the Erechtheion, proposing a bold theory for a new location of this important classical Athenian landmark on the basis of a rereading of a textual source (Jeppesen 1987). One of the last papers he ever published even offered a "fresh approach to the problems of the Parthenon frieze" (Jeppesen 2007), yet another revered and much-discussed monument of classical Greek architectural sculpture.

Jeppesen's scholarly interests are furthermore evident in the small exhibition space that he constructed on the Mausoleum grounds, soon after the completion of the excavations in 1977.[8] It was officially opened in 1983 (*Maussolleion* 5, 8). Every single label, every single display, even the building itself was designed by Jeppesen. The Mausoleum museum thus constitutes a unique document to one scholar's vision of the Mausoleum and the practices of classicism that informed it. It has a dual function: One part houses the storerooms for Jeppesen's excavations, and the other exhibits the results of the Mausoleum excavations to visitors. The exhibition focuses primarily on architecture and secondarily on (architectural) sculpture, displaying significant architectural fragments unearthed in Jeppesen's excavations, parts of the Amazon frieze discovered in the castle, and casts of those now in the British Museum. Only two pieces of the large amounts of pottery unearthed in the Mausoleum excavations are on display. Long didactic texts in Turkish and English explain the highly technical issues relating to the reconstruction of individual parts of the monument itself, as well as its place within the history of classical Greek architecture. The museum also houses three-dimensional models of the urban layout of ancient Halikarnassos and the Mausoleum, which will be discussed in more detail below. The only attempt made to tell the long-term history and significance of the site consists of a series of photographs of Euro-American classicising architecture. This privileging of a particular past – in this case, the fourth century BC and its Western afterlife – is typical of European archaeological projects working in the Mediterranean, at least until very recent times. No attempt is made to place the monument within its longer ancient history or more modern, Turkish context. The sense of isolation from the outside world that one encounters inside the museum is further emphasised on the outside by the modern wall that surrounds the Mausoleum site. This wall was constructed to control access to the Mausoleum (and to charge visitors an admission fee) but has the palpable side effect of completely insulating it from its immediate environment.

Jeppesen's research agenda was firmly rooted in *Bauforschung* and its underlying ideological framework, in which classical Greek monuments are studied as possessing an eternal value and intrinsic importance. This can be observed both in his excavations of the Mausoleum and the museum that he constructed at the site. Early Danish fieldwork in Bodrum in this sense followed the long-term trajectory of the European colonisation of scholarship that has been intensively studied in many parts of the eastern Mediterranean, including other parts of Turkey (Özdoğan 1998), Greece (Hamilakis 2013) and Egypt (Meskell 2000, 2005). The informal colonial legacy of the project is indeed evident from the official title of his project, the Danish Archaeological Expedition to Bodrum, a title also used in the publications of the Mausoleum. The classical heritage produced through Jeppesen's excavations was in many ways a direct outcome of a particular habitus deeply rooted in Danish (and European) academia. The power to produce and define knowledge of the classical world did not lie in the hands of the countries of origin but was colonised by the European nations and their academic habitus (Hamilakis 2016, 2007, 57–125; Jezernik 2007). Thus, while the excavations took place in a complex modern geopolitical setting, they focused exclusively on producing knowledge that fitted within a paradigm developed in Europe in the nineteenth century and that fed into the Danish subscription to classicism. The next section looks in more detail at one significant example of this, namely Jeppesen's efforts to reconstruct the Mausoleum.

Reconstructing the wonder

The fact that the Mausoleum is a seemingly lost wonder of the ancient world has gripped the imagination of European scholars and artists for centuries. As in the case of other lost wonders of the ancient world, reconstruction is an occupation with remarkable longevity as well as considerable ingenuity. Literally hundreds of different reconstructions have been put forward in the past five centuries. Before Newton's excavations, these reconstructions were based entirely on the ancient texts for which they were sometimes intended as illustrations, as in the case of Cesariano's translation of Vitruvius, published in 1521. Newton himself did not publish a reconstruction of the Mausoleum, but several influential proposals were made by R. M. Smith and R. P. Pulland on the basis of his excavations (Bury 1998; *Maussolleion* 5, 210). These were later revised in an influential and very evocative reconstruction of the Mausoleum proposed by the German *Bauforscher* Fritz Krischen in a posthumously published volume that discussed and reconstructed every one of the seven wonders of the ancient world (Krischen 1956, 69–86). In light of the Mausoleum's poor state of preservation, engagement in such reconstruction work is a powerful example of imaginary geography at work in scholarly practices. Indeed, every proposed reconstruction of the Mausoleum blends in different ways fact with what will arguably always be some degree of fiction or fantasy.

In light of this persistent tradition of undertaking reconstruction, and indeed Jeppesen's background as an architect, it was only natural for him to propose new reconstructions of the Mausoleum. Indeed, we saw earlier how he had already proposed a series of reconstruction drawings of the Mausoleum in his 1958 dissertation (Figure 4.3). Jeppesen even cited the opportunity to re-evaluate Krischen's reconstruction as one of the main reasons to begin new excavations at the site of the Mausoleum (*Maussolleion* 1, 9). While Jeppesen's excavations were still ongoing, he published preliminary reports that included revised reconstructions and offered new, more detailed proposals of the Mausoleum (Jeppesen 1976, 57). As discussed above, the reconstruction of every possible architectural detail of the Mausoleum would occupy Jeppesen for the rest of his life. Through his own proposals, Jeppesen actively engaged in this scholarly game of reconstruction, even upping the stakes through the authority of his 11-year excavation campaign at the site of the Mausoleum. He was clearly aware that the crowning achievement of any archaeologist working on the Mausoleum was to propose a new, seemingly more accurate and persuasive reconstruction.[9] This is also clear from the fact that he collected photographs of the display of his reconstruction in museum exhibitions around the world.

Yet Jeppesen's attempt to reconstruct the Mausoleum was not only a scholarly practice confined to paper. As early as 1974, he had begun experimental work on a three-dimensional scale model of his reconstruction of the architecture and sculptural decoration of the Mausoleum (Jeppesen 1976, Taf. 14–15; *Maussolleion* 1, 18). This work continued for the next 25 years and produced one of the most significant, concrete legacies of the project, namely two 1:50 scale reconstruction models of the Mausoleum that are displayed both on site at the Mausoleum Museum in Bodrum and in the Museum of Ancient Art and Archaeology in Aarhus. Currently, the Aarhus model is displayed as an isolated monument in a glass case (Figure 4.4), whereas the Bodrum model is part of a larger display that also depicts the terrace on which it was located, thus giving a better sense of its placement

Figure 4.4 Jeppesen's Mausoleum reconstruction in the Museum of Ancient Art
    and Archaeology, Aarhus

Source: Photo courtesy of Troels Myrup Kristensen

within the larger urban setting intended by Maussollos (Figure 4.5).[10] Both models were made in collaboration with Aksel Sønderborg, who participated as technician in the Mausoleum excavations in 1967 and 1970. Sønderborg was trained as a cabinetmaker and had extensive experience working in a local furniture workshop before coming to the Museum of Ancient Art and Archaeology, where he stayed for 25 years until his retirement. A striking feature of Jeppesen and Sønderborg's Mausoleum model is how its materials and composition identify the origins of its makers. The choice of wood, the lack of added colour and the generally minimalist style of reconstruction thus display a distinctively Nordic aesthetic sensibility. At the same time, the model follows a general trend among such archaeological reconstruction models in preferring a generally minimalist style that signifies scientific objectivity.

Model-making has in fact a long history in relation to the study of the classical world, in which it has been used as an object of dissemination in museums and as a souvenir in private collections. Going back to sixteenth-century Italy, cork scale models were made of famous monuments, often depicting them in a romantic state of ruination, as imaginative reconstructions or some hybrid thereof (Kockel 1993, 1998). Travellers on the grand tour purchased many of these as souvenirs. The English architect John

Figure 4.5 Jeppesen's Mausoleum reconstruction in Mausoleum Museum, Bodrum

Source: Photo courtesy of Troels Myrup Kristensen

Soane (1753–1837) thus amassed a large collection of cork models, including Pompeii, Palmyra, the Temple of Vesta at Tivoli, and the Tower of the Winds at Athens, which are still on display in his London residence, along with his extensive collection of antiquities. In this case, the models offered a means through which a collector could lay some claim to ownership over monuments in foreign lands and of a size that was otherwise out of reach. The massive 1:250 plaster reconstruction of third-century-AD Rome begun by the archaeologist Italo Gismondi (1887–1974) for Mussolini's Museo della Civiltà Romana but not completed until 1971 is another influential model reconstruction. In this case, the monumental size and meticulous detail in the reconstruction of particular buildings were designed to awe the public and to induce a particular sense of nostalgia for the glorious past of imperial Rome that fitted into Fascist propaganda. Other models of Ostia and Villa Adriana were also undertaken by Gismondi and prominently displayed in Italian museums (Filippi 2007, 275–280). A similar three-dimensional plaster model of Lindos is on display in the Danish National Museum, where it functions as a didactic tool that gives visitors a sense of the dramatic landscape in which the Danish excavations operated and also reminds them of Danish scholarly claims to this Mediterranean island (see chapter 3). Scale models of this type offer many advantages. By their scaled-down nature, they allow for a bird's-eye view of monuments that would otherwise be difficult to grasp, and by presenting three-dimensional reconstructions, they allow viewers to understand better the original appearance of particular monuments. However, the practice of reconstruction was also a way of getting to grips with the occasional disappointment of confronting often rather meagre archaeological remains that rarely compare with the grandiose descriptions of them in ancient texts (Scott 2014, 274–275).

For Jeppesen, the practicalities involved in the making of a reconstruction model of the Mausoleum were a means of unlocking the difficult testimonies of the ancient textual sources and the results of his archaeological excavations, especially the hundreds of small architectural fragments unearthed, in line with the practical approaches so closely aligned with *Bauforschung*. Numerous revisions and tweaks were made to the models over the following 25 years while Jeppesen was preparing his final publication of the Mausoleum – a project that was not completed until 2002 (*Maussolleion* 5). It thus continued to be a work in progress, as a model of experimentation, refinement, trial and error. The model offered him an experimental tool to explore the detailed and highly technical questions that he had set out to ask about the reconstruction of the building's original appearance and sculptural decoration. This comes out in a discussion of work on the model that he undertook between 1987 and 1989, the outcome of which was a version he dubbed the "Cambridge-Uppsala model" (Jeppesen 1992, 1999, 53). This model helped him to make sense of the problems he had encountered in trying to combine the different sources: "When I had the opportunity to proceed experimentally by means of a three-dimensional model . . . it proved possible to interpret these sources of evidence in terms making complimentary sense" (*Maussolleion* 5, 7). In this way, the model embodies the totality of the archaeological knowledge produced by Jeppesen's work on the Mausoleum, by turning immaterial knowledge into a material object.

Yet Jeppesen also exploited the visual appeal of the Mausoleum model in other ways. On several occasions, it acted as an evocative stand-in for the hole in the ground where the Mausoleum had stood. Through its display in both Bodrum and Aarhus, the model constitutes some of the most direct hands-on heritage that emerged from Jeppesen's excavations. It furthermore plays a leading role in several of Jeppesen's publications. It served, for example, as the frontispiece of his 2002 volume on the superstructure of the Mausoleum, his final contribution to the series (*Maussolleion* 5). The model in this case is visually framed as the climax of his research on the Mausoleum. It stood in for the invisibility of the Mausoleum, offering a more effective tool of communication than the two-dimensional drawings that dominated the more technical archaeological reports stemming from the excavations. The model plays a similar role in popularising work on the Mausoleum. A local Aarhus newspaper used an illustration of the model in an article published in 1980, with a caption reading: "Model of the Mausoleum, built by Aksel Sønderborg, on the basis of the results of the Danish expedition. Now for the first time since antiquity one gets a complete picture of how this world wonder looked" (Garde 1980). The model thus offered two things – a unique and previously unavailable sense of completion, as well as a solution to an archaeological puzzle, a metaphor that Jeppesen uses himself in the accompanying interview in reference to the process of working on the Mausoleum.

The more general appeal of the archaeological imagination embedded in the practice of model-making was not lost on him either. An interview with the newspaper *Jyllands-Posten* dating to February 1999 is particularly revealing in this regard. The interview is littered with the common archaeological tropes of mystery, secrets and riddles unearthed from the ground through archaeological excavation. In the interview, Jeppesen expressed some of his aspirations for his excavations: "My wish was and is to get to the bottom of the secrets that lie buried here. I decided that I wanted to reconstruct the main features of this building [i.e. the Mausoleum], as far as it was possible" (Nyholm 1999, 2). The caption underneath the photo of Jeppesen that shows him on-site in the tomb chamber of Mausollos reads:

The Danish archaeologist Kristian Jeppesen loves to solve riddles and enthusiastically engages with the riddles that others believe to be unsolvable. He believes that he has solved about 80 per cent of the riddle [of reconstructing the Mausoleum] and he has built a model that can be seen in the museum in Bodrum.

(Nyholm 1999, 2)

The model – and by implication the archaeological site of the Mausoleum itself – is here, again, framed as a puzzle that has been solved by the detective archaeologist, a common trope in the public perception of archaeological practice (Holtorf 2007, 75–83).

In the early 2000s, Jeppesen again turned to the issue of reconstructing the Mausoleum, but this time on an altogether larger scale. In cooperation with the Danish architect Johannes Exner (1926–2015), he proposed a full-size reconstruction of the Mausoleum in its original location. Although this project has so far not been realised, it is testimony to some of the issues that currently face the Mausoleum, such as how to preserve the site for the future, as well as how to present its relatively meagre remains as one of the wonders of the ancient world. Indeed Jeppesen and Exner's reconstruction proposal hinted at future projects to come. Since 2017, a local foundation called the Akdeniz Ülkeleri Akademisi Vakfı (officially translated as the Mediterranean Countries Academy Foundation) has thus taken up some of their ideas and is actively promoting the reconstruction of the Mausoleum to its full original height, using glass and steel, citing Jeppesen as one of the originators of their reconstruction proposal.[11] The explicit aim of the new project is to restore the grandeur of Bodrum's past and to reclaim the city's role as home to one of the wonders of the ancient world. Jeppesen's wooden model hinted at such possibilities, but is clearly not sufficient for the ambitions of Bodrum in the twenty-first century. Reconstruction is thus once again much more than a trivial matter. It plays into contemporary ambitions about the use of archaeology for local and national identity construction.

Beyond the Mausoleum

This final section looks briefly at Danish fieldwork in Bodrum since the completion of the Mausoleum excavations in 1977, in order to discuss how the nature and interpretive framework of this work is indicative of the changing academic and political landscapes in which it operates. The ongoing fieldwork certainly highlights changes in archaeological practice, but it is equally reflective of the increasingly uneasy relationship between two fundamentally different imagined geographies. On the one side, we can observe a continued Danish investment in archaeological fieldwork that is deeply rooted in classicism, and a particular conception of classical heritage that attracted Jeppesen and many other European scholars to the Mediterranean in the first place. On the other hand, we have the contemporary politics of the Turkish Republic, since 2003 under the leadership of Recep Tayyip Erdoğan's Justice and Development Party (JDP), which has applied a nationalistic and increasingly neo-Ottoman agenda in its approach to heritage sites and monuments (Aykaç 2018; Bozoğlu and Whitehead, forthcoming). In response to the complex accession talks and the ongoing refugee crisis, the relationship between Turkey and the EU has become increasingly strained in recent years. All of these developments have important implications for the contexts in which archaeological knowledge is produced. During the 50-year period that Danish archaeologists have been active in Bodrum, public and political expectations of archaeological scholarship have thus changed dramatically, in Turkey and in Denmark, as well as in Europe more broadly (Human 2015).

Poul Pedersen, who after 1970 had worked closely with Jeppesen, was the first scholar to expand the Danish fieldwork to the wider urban setting of ancient Halikarnassos (Table 4.1). Pedersen's initial work focused on the Mausoleum terrace and its place in the urban grid of Halikarnassos, which was part of Maussollos's refoundation of the city (*Maussolleion* 3; Pedersen 1999a, 1999b). He later expanded to areas further beyond the Mausoleum, including the defensive walls that circle the city, and the Salmakis fountain, an important monument that celebrated the mythical foundation of Halikarnassos (Isager and Pedersen 2004), as well as to the Zephyrion peninsula, where he attempted to locate the remains of Maussollos's palace and its "secret" harbour described by Vitruvius (Pedersen 2009). Pedersen's main interest lies in the study of Greek architecture, continuing the tradition of *Bauforschung*. His work focuses, for example, on the concept of the Ionian Renaissance, first developed by W. B. Dinsmoor in 1950 to describe the innovative architecture of fourth-century-BC western Asia Minor and its origins in the hybrid cultural environment at the intersection of the Greek and Persian worlds (Pedersen 1994). He thus also situated Halikarnassian developments in a larger social and cultural framework.

Since the 1970s, Danish fieldwork has investigated many parts of the increasingly urbanised landscape of Bodrum and has even covered the wider region of the peninsula, as in Anne Marie Carstens' surveys of Karian tombs and Hekatomnid ruler ideology (Carstens 2002, 2009). The fieldwork has never followed a masterplan but developed in an ad hoc fashion as new opportunities appeared, always working in close cooperation with Turkish archaeologists at the Bodrum Museum of Underwater Archaeology. Notably, in the early 1990s, Birte Poulsen excavated a late Roman

Table 4.1 Overview of Danish archaeological projects in Bodrum

1966–1977	Excavations of the Maussolleion
1978–ongoing	Topographical research in the city of Halikarnassos
1988	Geophysical investigations by the Doric Stoa and the Temple of Mars
1990–1993	Excavations of the House of Charidemos
1991	Excavation of Hellenistic house
1991–ongoing	Investigations of inscriptions from Halikarnasssos
1992–1993, 2002–2004	Excavations in the castle (Palace of Maussollos)
1995	Investigations of the Salmakis fountain
1998–2000, 2013–2014	Investigations of the city walls, Myndos gate and Late Antique necropolis

Source: Compiled by Jakob Munk Højte

complex (the so-called House of Charidemos, currently in its publication phase), and she later turned her attention to a Late Antique necropolis outside the Myndos gate in the western part of the modern city (Mortensen and Poulsen 2016). Both projects were initiated in response to rescue excavations. The studies that have appeared based on this work, while often following long-standing paradigms of classicism, demonstrate a broadening of scholarly interests both in their temporal and theoretical scope, addressing much more explicitly, for example, questions relating to social and cultural history across the *longue durée*. The change in focus from individual monuments to broader urban dynamics also reflects changes within the discipline of classical archaeology more generally that are also apparent in the case of other Euro-American projects in Turkey, such as, for example, Ephesus and Sagalassos. They also reflect the changing discourses around classicism in the classroom (see chapter 2) and museums more broadly (see chapter 3), noticeably by engaging in issues such as the meeting of cultures. Postcolonial perspectives have thus been introduced to rectify the frequent tendency in European scholarship to look at Karia (and western Asia Minor more generally) from an exclusively Greek perspective (Davis 2003, 160), addressing at least some of the concerns about European biases that are seen in the writings of the Fisherman of Halikarnassos.

The 50th anniversary of Danish fieldwork in Bodrum was celebrated with an exhibition that opened in the Museum of Ancient Art and Archaeology in Aarhus in 2016. The Bodrum project indeed has a special place in Danish archaeology as the longest-running project outside the country's borders. Yet since 2014, no permission has been issued by the Turkish authorities for Danish archaeologists to work in Bodrum, in parallel with the plight of many other international teams that are increasingly experiencing similar difficulty in obtaining permissions to carry out excavations. The situation has been summarised bluntly by Peter Thonemann in a recent review of a new volume on the results of Late Antique archaeological projects in Asia Minor:

> Over the past few years, the political climate in Turkey has become increasingly hostile to European archaeologists, and many of the innovative fieldwork projects summarised in this volume have been shut down by Turkish authorities on the flimsiest of pretexts. The priorities of the Turkish Ministry of Culture and Tourism are explicitly driven by the aesthetic preferences of revenue-bearing foreign tourists, and gleaming white marble columns are back at the top of the agenda.
>
> (Thonemann 2018, 262)

While we should object to the tone of Thonemann's remarks and its underlying colonial ironies, his comments capture well the sense of two sets of imagined geographies that are increasingly finding themselves on collision course.

Worlds apart?

To paraphrase the title of David Lowenthal's seminal work (Lowenthal 1985), to Danish classicists, the past may well be a foreign country, but it will very literally always be located in a foreign country, with all of the social, economic and political ramifications that this entails. In their movements across modern borders, their engagements with local authorities, and with financial and institutional support from their home country, Danish archaeologists have thus operated within a very particular imagined geography, with the seemingly objective aims of recovering and reconstructing classical heritage, following a long-running tradition of European archaeology that goes back to the eighteenth century. This chapter has traced some of the trajectories of Danish archaeological fieldwork in Bodrum and how through its ongoing excavations and publication projects it has produced a specific kind of academic capital. Jeppesen's excavation and reconstruction of the Mausoleum, a wonder of the ancient world, is one of the most significant outcomes of this particular kind of classicism. Increasingly, however, the academic habitus that can be observed in Jeppesen's work (and some of his successors) is being challenged by postcolonial perspectives within the discipline, as well as by significant shifts in contemporary international politics. In some ways, the archaeological fieldwork in Bodrum offered an opportunity to recentre Danish classicism away from the Othering that is inherent in many European engagements with Turkey (Wintle 2016), but this potential has so far not been fully realised.

Notes

1 Turkish perspectives on this fieldwork will be discussed in forthcoming publications from the CoHERE project.

2 Notable examples include the tower of St George's, Bloomsbury, London (1730); the House of the Temple, Washington DC (1911–1915); the Los Angeles City Hall (1926–1928); and the Shrine of Remembrance, Melbourne (1927–1934).

3 This was just one of the exhibition's references to classical architecture; among others were a triumphal arch and a victory column closely referencing those of Trajan and Marcus Aurelius in Rome. On the exhibition and its reception of classical antiquity, see Nørskov (2008, 19–21).

4 These institutes remain important to the disciplinary infrastructure of the study of the ancient world, facilitating fieldwork and maintaining important libraries as well as being involved in a range of research and training activities (for a critique, see Shanks 1996). The Danes were relative latecomers to this practice, with their first such institute opening in 1956 in Rome, followed by another in 1992 in Athens and, most recently, in 2000 in Damascus.

5 In this context, it is worth noting that the introduction of prehistory in Danish universities was a later development, with an associate professorship in Nordic archaeology not being filled until 1929. It was not until 1941 that the first professorship in Nordic and European Prehistory was occupied (Johansen 1943, 166). Since 1949, classical archaeology has also been taught at Aarhus University, a relatively new university founded in 1928.

6 This work in fact extends as far as the Arabian Gulf, not least thanks to the efforts of P. V. Glob (1911–1985) (Højlund 1999). Jeppesen participated in Glob's expedition to the island of Failaka, Kuwait, where he excavated a small Hellenistic period temple (published as Jeppesen 1989).

7 Important to the archaeology of Bodrum is also the town's sponge diving community, which identified numerous underwater archaeological finds, in turn attracting foreign archaeologists. The Institute of Nautical Archaeology, founded in 1973 by George Bass, thus has a presence in the town stretching back to the 1960s.

8 A project to preserve and exhibit the Mausoleum to the public was sketched as early as October 1975. This project aimed to cover the entire site with a large roof of 35 by 40 m. According to the plan, which was not fully realised, visitors would be allowed to enter the Mausoleum, including the tomb chamber itself. The Mausoleum museum was sponsored by the Danish International Development Agency (Danida) and the Turkish Ministry of Culture.

9 As evident also in his attacks on competing reconstructions, see *Maussolleion* 5, 15–18, 207–218. As expected, Jeppesen's reconstruction has not been accepted by all scholars. Most recently it was critiqued in a popular book by Wolfram Hoepfner (2013).

10 Originally the Aarhus model was also placed in a larger setting with an indication of the extent of the temenos.

11 The plans were officially presented at the Mausoleum International Workshop in Bodrum, 5–6 May 2017. For information on the work of the foundation, see www.academia.org.tr.

5 Becoming European

The critical heritage of Danish classicism

This book has explored how disparate agents and institutions have used classical heritage in a range of different contexts to construct a particular European identity within the Danish nation state, sometimes through explicit agendas and discourses, at other times through subtler, more deeply ingrained practices. Many of the issues covered in previous chapters converge in the case of a special exhibition at the National Museum in Copenhagen that was organised to celebrate the Danish presidency of the Council of the EU in 2012 (Figure 5.1). Entitled "Europe Meets the World," the exhibition was opened on 12 January with the participation of the Danish Prime Minister Helle Thorning Schmidt and the President of the European Commission José Manuel Barroso.[1] The first object that visitors encountered in the exhibition was a fragment of an Attic red-figure vase depicting the Phoenician princess Europa on a bull, once again turning to classical antiquity as the foundation of Europe. Barroso picked up on the choice of this vase in his speech, remarking that "during this period of your Presidency, you can personally meet Europe at the beginning of this exhibition." He furthermore pointed to culture and civilisation as the core values of Europe, staying true to the tropes of classicism that we have encountered throughout this book.

The exhibition, chronologically organised into nine themes, rhetorically and materially configured Denmark's position within Europe, culturally as well as geographically. The small-scale geography of the exhibition thus mirrored the large-scale imagined geography that points to classical antiquity as Europe's foundation. The ancient etymology of the continent's name (as evoked by the representation of a Phoenician princess on a 2500-year old Greek piece of pottery) was followed by a section on ancient Athens entitled "The story begins", reminding us of the choice of words in the European Heritage label encountered on the Athenian acropolis (Figure 1.1). This section included a portrait of Socrates, framed here as the first free spirit in history and described as a young rebel, the wisest of all (Rasmussen and Lund 2012, 35–36). Facing Socrates was a portrait of Alexander

Figure 5.1 The classical past in the exhibition "Europe Meets the World" at the National Museum in Copenhagen 2012. Socrates faces Alexander the Great

Source: Photo courtesy of John Lee, The National Museum of Denmark, CC-BY-SA

the Great, framed as the embodiment of cultural encounter as a key element of European identity and as part of a theme entitled "Towards new horizons", signalling the geographical and cultural expansion of the Greek world during the Hellenistic period (Kjeldbæk 2012, 421). Rome featured as a superpower but also as a multicultural empire as both a consequence and requirement of its vast geographical expanse, exemplified by the many ethnicities and cultures represented in its army (Rasmussen *et al*. 2012). The fall of the Roman Empire was presented as a time of crisis for European coherence, which left Christianity as the sole "unifying bearer of culture" (Kjeldbæk 2012, 424) – a rather crass remark in the context of an increasingly multicultural and multireligious Europe as well as the cultural complexities of the late antique world, not least in the Middle East.

Responses to the exhibition in Danish media were varied. In *Berlingske Tidende*, the historian Bent Blüdnikow gave the exhibition three out of six stars and described it as "neat, nice, and as predictable as an upper secondary school essay" (2012), pointing in particular to its failure to address the antagonistic and diverse heritages of European history in a meaningful way. Blüdnikow furthermore implied that the exhibition's use and conceptualisation of Greek and Roman heritage was predictable given the naturalised and consolidated role of these heritages in the Danish relation to

Europe and European identity. Blüdnikow's response is interesting for what it reveals about how the premise of the exhibition – that the roots of European civilisation are to be found in classical antiquity – could be taken as a matter of course. That assumption highlights a key aspect of what we have been pursuing in this volume: that is, to trace how such tropes have become naturalised through the practices of Danish classicism – ranging from school education to museum visits and even a very particular and singular type of academic habitus.

Although these practices, and the underlying tropes that support them, have a very long and varied history (in Denmark as well as in Europe more broadly), the case studies in this book pinpoint a quite narrow period when this narrative was manifested on a new, institutionalised scale. Just after the turn of the twentieth century, a pivotal moment in Denmark's imagined geography can indeed be identified. The launch of the Lindos excavations in 1902 ushered in a new, ambitious era of Danish excavations in the Mediterranean, starting a long-term tradition of seeking out material remains from the age of classical antiquity, a tradition sponsored predominantly by private means but enacted by professors and curators in state institutions. In 1903, Classical Studies (*Oldtidskundskab*) was introduced in upper secondary schools, leading to a development that would see a much larger proportion of the Danish population being introduced to Greek and Roman culture than in the previous century. Three years later, in 1906, the classical collections in the Ny Carlsberg Glyptotek opened their doors, making one of the world's most important assemblages of classical sculpture available to the general public in a context where it was contextualised as the predecessor of later European (and Danish) art. The collection, together with that of the National Museum, materialised Danish claims to the imagined geography of classical heritage, as Ussing made clear in his memoirs. Over this short span of just four years, classical antiquity was thus both materialised and consolidated as part of Danish cultural heritage on a new, larger scale and on a much stronger foundation than during the nineteenth century where it was tied to a small elite. The institutionalisation of the classical as a constituent element in Denmark's imagined geography has indeed been paramount for the continued preservation and promulgation of classicism through formal education and heritage.

The moment falls in a period of transformation. The Danish democracy finally had a liberal government elected in 1901, the first without royal interference, thus establishing parliamentarianism as the principle of government. Industrialisation had provided economic growth, technology had changed mobility and communication, and Europe had become "closer" and within reach of the general public. Ideologically the consolidation of classicism was tied to notions of *Bildung* and the formation of the Danish citizen as a democratic subject in a modern European nation state. Denmark placed itself in the European and especially German tradition of Hellenism, conceptualising classical Greece not only as an example of culture at its peak but as the European foundation on which central values in Danish culture and society rested. Another movement in this cultural melting pot in which key elements of modern European identities developed was vitalism, both an epoch in its own right (1890–1940) and a current feeding into twentieth-century modernism (Hvidberg-Hansen and Oelsner 2011, 14–17). Vitalism was interested in health, beauty and strength and constitutes a form of classicism that has been rather neglected, probably because it articulated some of the ideological baggage of Fascism and Nazism in the twentieth century. Nevertheless, it could be argued that thinking in this period, with classical antiquity as its role model and an understanding of art and nature as organically intertwined, contributed decisively to the naturalisation of the classical as the foundation for Danish culture.

In our explorations of the three case studies, the meanings and appropriations of the classical by a number of actors and institutions have shown an increased naturalisation of distinct classical heritages during the periods investigated. This process laid the foundation for the shape and message of the "Europe Meets the World" exhibition more than 100 years later. Chapter 2 explored the establishment of the subject Classical Studies as a foundation for knowledge about Greek culture in the education of an increasing proportion of the Danish population. Focusing on canonical texts by Homer and Plato, Greek mythology and thinking have become internalised in the conceptualisation of the Danish European (as the current Minister of Culture indeed reminded us in chapter one). Chapter 3 looked at the display of classical antiquities in two major collections in Copenhagen, where it became evident how museum communication and education have substantiated the narrative of the classical as the foundation of European identity and in this way placed Denmark within a larger, imagined geography of Europe. Finally, chapter 4 turned to Danish fieldwork in the Mediterranean, and Turkey more specifically, in order to establish how such work was informed by the practices of classicism. Investments in fieldwork overseas – by both private and public sponsors – can be translated into cultural capital and thus qualify Denmark as a European power within academia.

In Denmark's case, the dissemination of the narrative of classicism is contingent on – and to a great extent formed by – agents and institutions that span professionals, public and private actors. The professional field embodied by archaeologists, philologists and classicists supplies the employees of both secondary schools and museums, thus making a division between professionals and public less evident. The professional voice in the public debate on the role of classical antiquity has been extremely powerful in the negotiations over the role of classical heritage as link to a European communality. A strong intellectual elite still dictates the discourses on the role of the classical in Denmark. However, the democratisation of the classical through the subject of Classical Studies provides a much broader foundation to speak from and to. This also explains the Danish People's Party's support for the preservation of the classical as essential, in spite of its antipathy towards the EU. Danish Classicism is thus enshrined both as a core element in Danish identity and as a link to European culture and ideals more broadly.

The increased focus on a culture-historical understanding of the classical world has imbued the imagined geography of ancient Greece and Rome with a relativistic, organic idea of culture. This narrative makes it possible to fuse the imagined geographies of Denmark, Europe and the ancient world two times over – in the past, and in the present. In the first instance, the narrative of cultural exchange illustrates how elements of classical culture made their way across Europe to Denmark so as to become part of Danish cultural history. The perceived central qualities of classical culture take on a universal character that not only defines them, but places them in a cultural continuum defining Europe across time and space. Subsequently, through appropriations and receptions, classical antiquity continues to define European culture precisely because it represents a core cultural trait. The central values ascribed to classical antiquity are cultural exchange as a precondition for European/global civilisation, but also democratic and critical values. These are the values sustained by contemporary museum displays and found in the advocacy of the continuing relevance of Classical Studies, which argues that the study of classical antiquity prepares students for the reality of globalisation in the present.

The case studies have shown a dichotomy between a universal conceptualisation of the classical as European heritage in the singular, and a fluctuating emphasis on the diversity of classical heritages. In the latter case, while the main divide is whether the classical is to be defined predominantly as Greek or Roman, a third idea of the classical has emerged: the idea of classical antiquity as multicultural, even global. This new conceptualisation has challenged the established imagined geographies of classical antiquity as a specific cultural realm limited to Europe and the Mediterranean. This opens up the possibility of new futures for the field, while also potentially raising new questions about universalism – or, even better, by questioning universalism altogether. This is clear above all in the case of Turkey, where European archaeologists have increasingly become frustrated in their efforts to secure excavation permits as well as to present their finds in ways that have been regarded as universal for more than a century. Such changes in the geopolitical landscape pose challenges to classicism but also opportunities to revisit the discipline's history, its fault lines and inherent biases.

Challenges to classicism have been met by arguments relating to the threat of cultural marginalisation instead of reflections on the broader question of the concept of culture that is being challenged. The repetition of the tropes of democracy, critical thought and the aesthetics of primarily classical Athens becomes an act of appropriation of imagined places and pasts, resulting in a singular conception of identity. This appropriation excludes certain narratives of classical antiquity, for example, of slavery, gender roles and aggressive imperialism, sanitising these parts of European heritage to the point where it is beyond critique. Sustaining this narrative not only fuels potentially dangerous narratives of Western cultural superiority and "Othering", but also runs the risk of cultural imperialism within the borders of Europe denying the influence and agency of other past cultures as part of the cultural matrix that constitutes Europe today.

Recent political and cultural developments, with increasing economic and social mobility and globalisation at their centre, are profoundly changing the concept of Europe as a coherent, homogenous cultural entity. Acknowledgement of the rapidly changing political and cultural conditions within and outside Europe has furthermore resulted in a need within Europe, and especially within the EU's institutions, to seek out and define an especially "European" identity for the twenty-first century. It is this kind of agenda that the "Europe meets the World" exhibition responded to, in a way that can be said to be paradigmatic of how Danish institutions have used classical heritage to construct a particular imagined geography that places Denmark within Europe. At the European level this agenda is further promoted by the award of the European Heritage Label to classical Athens and its monuments as well as within the House of European History in Brussels in which the imagined geography of classical antiquity still holds considerable resonance as a shared European past. Yet such a monolithic narrative frequently leaves too little space for dissonance and for a critical approach to classical heritage to emerge, in turn creating blind spots and an unhealthy resilience towards changes in discourse and approach. The pressing question now is how this new Europe will reframe its classical past in order to reflect its contemporary challenges.

Note

1 Barroso's talk: http://ec.europa.eu/avservices/video/player.cfm?sitelang=EN& ref=I071997 (accessed 19 June 2018).

Bibliography

Adams, M. (2015) *Teaching Classics in English Schools, 1500–1840*, Newcastle: Cambridge Scholars Publishing.

Afzelius, A. (1950) 'Græsk litteratur i dansk oversættelse', *Nordisk tidsskrift för vetenskap, konst och industri* 26, 134–139.

Alpözen, O. (1983) 'The Bodrum Museum of Underwater Archaeology', *Museum International* 35.1, 61–63.

Andersen, F.G. (2000) 'De lovbefalede klassikere', *Klassikerforeningens Meddelelser* 192, 9–23.

Andersen, J.K. (1985) 'Egocentri', in H. Bolt-Jørgensen *et al.* (eds.) *Her kan vi se vores egne Vinduer – humaniora i gymnasiet*, Hjørring: Klassikerforeningens kildehæfter, pp. 47–50.

Anderson, B. (2015) '"An Alternative Discourse": Local Interpreters of Antiquities in the Ottoman Empire', *Journal of Field Archaeology* 40.4, 450–460.

Anderson, B. (2016) *Imagined Communities: Reflections on the Origin and Spread of Nationalism*, revised edition, London: Verso.

Andreasen, B. (2003) *Om fortidens fremtid. Forsvarstaler for det klassiske*, Aarhus: Aarhus Universitetsforlag.

Antiksamlingen (1950) *Oriental and Classical Antiquity: Egypt, western Asia, Greece and Rome*, Copenhagen: The National Museum.

Antiksamlingen (1968) *Greece, Italy and the Roman Empire*, Copenhagen: The National Museum.

Aronson, P. (2011) 'Explaining National Museums: Exploring Comparative Approaches to the Study of National Museums', in S. Knell, P. Aronson and A.B. Amundsen (eds.) *National Museums: New Studies from around the World*, London: Routledge, pp. 29–54.

Arthurs, J. (2012) *Excavating Modernity: The Roman Past in Fascist Italy*, Ithaca: Cornell University Press.

Aykaç, P. (2018) 'Musealisation as a Strategy for the Reconstruction of an Idealised Ottoman Past: Istanbul's Sultanahmet District as a "Museum-Quarter"', *International Journal of Heritage Studies*. Online: https://doi.org/10.1080/13527258.20 18.1475407

Bager, P. (1985) 'Filosofi i gymnasiet', in H. Bolt-Jørgensen *et al.* (eds.) *Her kan vi se vores egne Vinduer – humaniora i gymnasiet*, Hjørring: Klassikerforeningens kildehæfter, pp. 85–88.

Baker, P. (2015) *Italian Renaissance Humanism in the Mirror*, Cambridge: Cambridge University Press.

Bang, P.F. (ed.) (2005) *Fremmed og moderne. Glimt af antikken i Europa*, Aarhus: Aarhus Universitetsforlag.

Barkan, L. (1999) *Unearthing the Past: Archaeology and Aesthetics in the Making of Renaissance Culture*, New Haven and London: Yale University Press.

Beard, M. and J. Henderson (1995) *Classics: A Very Short Introduction*, Oxford: Oxford University Press.

Bekendtgørelse om Undervisning i gymnasiet 1906, 4.12, nr. 265. Online: http://library.au.dk/uploads/tx_lfskolelov/1906-12-04_265.pdf (accessed 22 June 2018).

Bekendtgørelse om undervisning I gymnasiet 1971, 16.6., nr. 322. Online: http://library.au.dk/uploads/tx_lfskolelov/1971_06_16.pdf (accessed 22 June 2018).

Bender, J. (2008) *Hurra for Århus! Landsudstillingen 1909 – vejene til og sporene fra*, Aarhus: Klematis.

Bender, J., H. Bolt-Jørgensen, F. Jorsal, A.-G. Kristiansen and G. Torresin (1981) *Oldtidskundskab*, Hjørring: Klassikerforeningens kildehæfter.

Bendtsen, M. (1993) *Sketches and Measurings: Danish Architects in Greece 1818–1862*, Aarhus: Aarhus University Press.

Berry, H. (2009) 'Regional Identity and Material Culture', in K. Harvey (ed.) *History and Material Culture: A Student's Guide to Approaching Alternative Sources*, London: Routledge, pp. 139–157.

Bilde, P.G. (2000) 'From Study Collection to the Museum of Ancient Art: A Danish University Museum of Mediterranean Antiquities and Plaster Casts', in J. Lund and P. Pentz (eds.) *Between Orient and Occident: Studies in Honour of P.J. Riis*, Copenhagen: The National Museum, pp. 209–231.

Bilsel, C. (2012) *Antiquity on Display: Regimes of the Authentic in Berlin's Pergamon Museum*, Oxford: Oxford University Press.

Blinkenberg, C. (1941) 'De danske Udgravninger i Lindos', in *Arkæologiske og Kunsthistoriske Afhandlinger tilegnede Frederik Poulsen 7.3.1941*, Copenhagen: Gyldendalske Boghandel Nordisk Forlag, pp. 1–14.

Blüdnikow, B. (2012) 'Ingen smæk for skillingen på Europa-udstilling', *Berlingske Tidende* 17 January.

Bolt-Jørgensen, H. (2003) 'Prolog til læserne', in H. Bolt-Jørgensen, I. Gjørup, S. Høeg, F. Jorsal, K.E. Staugaard and C.G. Tortzen (eds.) *Levende ord. Græsk, latin og oldtidskundskab*, Hjørring: Klassikerforeningens kildehæfter, pp. 7–12.

Bolt-Jørgensen, H., I. Gjørup, S. Høeg, F. Jorsal, K.E. Staugaard and C.G. Tortzen (eds.) (2003) *Levende ord. Græsk, latin og oldtidskundskab*, Hjørring: Klassikerforeningens kildehæfter.

Bolt-Jørgensen, H., C. Iuul, F. Jorsal and C.G. Tortzen (eds.) (1985) *Her kan vi se vores egne Vindver – humaniora i gymnasiet*, Hjørring: Klassikerforeningens kildehæfter.

Bolter, J. (1980) 'Friedrich August Wolf and the Scientific Study of Antiquity', *Greek, Roman, and Byzantine Studies* 2, 83–99.

Bonini Baraldi, S., D. Shoup and L. Zan (2013) 'Understanding Cultural Heritage in Turkey: Institutional Context and Organisational Issues', *International Journal of Heritage Studies* 19.7, 728–748.

108   *Bibliography*

Bozoğlu, G. and C. Whitehead (forthcoming) 'Turkish Neo-Ottoman Memory Culture and the Problems of Copying the Past'.

Bradley, M. (ed.) (2010) *Classics and Imperialism in the British Empire*, Oxford: Oxford University Press.

Broval, S. (2016) 'Glyptoteket om udlevering af stjålen kunstskat: "Vi er blevet klogere"', *Politiken* 6 July.

Bury, J. (1998) 'Chapter III of the Hypnerotomachia Poliphili and the Tomb of Mausolus', *Word and Image* 14.1–2, 40–60.

Carlsen, J. (2003) 'Det antikke Rom: symbol og underholdning', in B. Andreasen (ed.) *Om fortidens fremtid – Forsvarstaler for det klassiske*, Aarhus: Aarhus Universitetsforlag, pp. 28–41.

Carstens, A.M. (2002) 'Tomb Cult on the Halikarnassos Peninsula', *American Journal of Archaeology* 106, 391–409.

Carstens, A.M. (2009) *Karia and the Hekatomnids: The Creation of a Dynasty*, Oxford: BAR International Series.

Christensen, L.K., P. Grinder-Hansen, E. Kjeldbæk and B.B. Rasmussen (2012) 'Introduction', in *Europe Meets the World*, Copenhagen: The National Museum, pp. 12–13.

Christiansen, J. (2000) *I lyset fra Akropolis. Danmark og Grækenland i 1800-tallet*, Copenhagen: Ny Carlsberg Glyptotek.

Christiansen, J. (2004) 'En hundredeårsfødselar', *Carlsbergfondet – Årsskrift 2004*, Copenhagen, pp. 132–141.

Christiansen, J. (2006) 'Museet og kulturhistorien. Etruskersamlingen', in F. Friborg and A.M. Nielsen (eds.) *Ny Carlsberg Glyptotek i Tiden*, Copenhagen: Ny Carlsberg Glyptotek, pp. 55–62.

Christiansen, J. (2008) *Middelhavshorisonten – en rejse gennem tiden – over havet*, Copenhagen: Ny Carlsberg Glyptotek.

Cook, B.F. (1997) 'Sir Charles Newton, KCB (1816–1894)', in I. Jenkins and G.B. Waywell (eds.) *Sculptors and Sculpture of Caria and the Dodecanese*, London: British Museum Press, pp. 10–23.

Cuno, J. (2008) *Who Owns Antiquity?*, Princeton: Princeton University Press.

Cuno, J. (ed.) (2012) *Whose Culture?: The Promise of Museums and the Debate over Antiquities*, Princeton: Princeton University Press.

Daugbjerg, M. (2011) 'Kulturarvens grundspænding mellem nationale og globale strømme', *Kulturstudier* 1, 6–35.

Davis, J.L. (2003) 'A Foreign School of Archaeology and the Politics of Archaeological Practice: Anatolia, 1922', *Journal of Mediterranean Archaeology* 16.2, 145–172.

Delanty, G. (2013) *Formations of European Modernity: A Historical and Political Sociology of Europe*, New York: Palgrave Macmillan.

Díaz-Andreu, M. (2001) 'Guest Editor's Introduction: Natonalism and Archaeology', *Nations and Nationalism* 7.4, 429–440.

Díaz-Andreu, M. (2007) *A World History of Nineteenth-Century Archaeology: Nationalism, Colonialism, and the Past*, Oxford: Oxford University Press.

Dietz, S. (ed.) (1999) *Det lykkelige Arkadien. Grækenland og Europa i 1700-tallet*, Copenhagen: Ny Carlsberg Glyptotek.

Dietz, S. and S. Trolle (1974) *Arkæologens Rhodos*, Copenhagen: Nationalmuseet.

Dyggve, E. (1960) *Lindos. Fouille de l'Acropole 1902–1914 et 1952, Volume III, I. Le Sanctuaire d'Athana Lindia et l'Architecture lindienne*, Berlin: Walter de Gruyter.

Dyson, S.L. (2006) *In Pursuit of Ancient Pasts: A History of Classical Archaeology in the Nineteenth and Twentieth Centuries*, New Haven: Yale University Press.

Ebbesen, S. (2016) 'Græsk er forståelsesnøglen til vores antikke rødder', *Kristeligt Dagblad*, Kroniken 16 January. Online: www.kristeligt-dagblad.dk/kronik/graesker-forstaaelsesnoeglen-til-vores-antikke-roedder (accessed 24 June 2018).

Elkjær, K. and P. Krarup (1947) *Danmark og antikken. En bibliografi*, København: Gyldendal.

Fakta (2015) *Fakta og myter om det almene gymnasium 2015*, København: Danske Gymnasier. Online: www.danskegymnasier.dk/wp-content/uploads/2014/11/Fakta-og-Myter-om-det-almene-gymnasium-2015.pdf (accessed 27 April 2018).

Federspiel, B.K. (2005) 'Institutionaliseringen af bevaringstanken i Danmark, Oldsagskommissionens kommissorium 1807', in B. Ingemann and A. Hejlskov Larsen (eds.) *Ny Dansk Museologi*, Aarhus: Aarhus Universitetsforlag, pp. 89–102.

Fejfer, J., A. Rathje and T. Fischer Hansen (eds.) (2003) *The Rediscovery of Antiquity: The Role of the Artist* (Acta Hyperborea 10), Copenhagen: Museum Tusculanum Press.

Feldbæk, O. (1991–1992) *Dansk Identitetshistorie*, Vol. 1–4, København: C.A. Reitzels Forlag.

Fich, H., T. Fischer Hansen, M. Moltesen and K. Waaben (1999) *Græsk kunst*, Copenhagen: Gads Forlag.

Filippi, F. (ed.) (2007) *Riconstruire l'Antico prima del virtuale. Italo Gismondi. Un architetto per l'archeologia (1887–1974)*, Rome: Archivio storico a Palazzo Altemps.

Fögen, T. and R. Warren (eds.) (2016) *Graeco-Roman Antiquity and the Idea of Nationalism in the 19th Century*, Berlin: De Gruyter.

Fouseki, K. (2014) 'Claiming the Parthenon Marbles Back: Whose Claim and on Behalf of Whom?', in L. Tythacott and K. Arvanitis (eds.) *Museums and Restitution: New Practices, New Approaches*, London and New York: Routledge, pp. 163–178.

Frevert, L. (2003) 'Question to the Minister of Education 14/3 03, S2436', Online: http://webarkiv.ft.dk/Samling/20021/spor_sv/S2436.htm (accessed 22 June 2018).

Friborg, F. (2006a) 'En skulpturmæcen i Danmark', in F. Friborg and A.M. Nielsen (eds.) *Ny Carlsberg Glyptotek i Tiden*, Copenhagen: Ny Carlsberg Glyptotek, pp. 9–14.

Friborg, F. (2006b) 'Om gaver og nødvendighed. Glyptotekets projekt 2006', in F. Friborg and A.M. Nielsen (eds.) *Ny Carlsberg Glyptotek i Tiden*, Copenhagen: Ny Carlsberg Glyptotek, pp. 179–191.

Friborg, F. (2007) 'Vil København ikke vide af Glyptoteket?', *Politiken* 16 October.

Friborg, F. et al. (2010) 'KULTURARV: Er KU ramt af globalt snæversyn?', *Politiken* 13 October.

110   *Bibliography*

Friborg, F. (1998) 'Carl Jacobsens Helligdomme', in F. Friborg, A.M. Nielsen and S. Roepstorff (eds.) *Carl Jacobsens Helligdomme*, Copenhagen: Ny Carlsberg Glyptotek, pp. 51–88.

Friborg, F. and Nielsen, A.M. (eds.) (2006) *Ny Carlsberg Glyptotek i Tiden*, Copenhagen: Ny Carlsberg Glyptotek.

Funder, L.M.A. (2014) *The Classical Narrative: A Study of the Reception of Classical Antiquity in Contemporary Europe through Analyses of the Narratives Produced by and Presented in Museum Exhibitions*, unpublished PhD thesis, Aarhus University.

Fürtwangler, A. (1893) *Meisterwerke der griechischen Plastik*, Leipzig: Giesecke & Devrient.

Gade, R. (2006) 'Hvad er udstillingsanalyse?', in E. Bodin and J. Lassenius (eds.) *Udstillinger – mellem fokus og flimmer*, Copenhagen: Multivers Academic, pp. 15–40.

Galmar, H. (1985) 'Oldtidskundskab og religion', in H. Bolt-Jørgensen *et al.* (eds.) *Her kan vi se vores egne Vinduer – humaniora i gymnasiet*, Hjørring: Klassikerforeningens kildehæfter, pp. 88–90.

Garde, C.F. (1980) 'Skål for kulturen i hele verden', *Aarhuus Stiftstidende* 29 November, 11.

Gill, D.W.J. and C. Chippindale (2007) 'From Malibu to Rome: Further Developments on the Return of Antiquities', *International Journal of Cultural Property* 14, 205–240.

Gjerløff, A.K. and A.F. Jacobsen (2014) *Da skolen blev sat i system. Dansk Skolehistorie, bind 3*. Aarhus: Aarhus Universitetsforlag.

Gjørup, I. (2003) 'Levende ord', in Henrik Bolt-Jørgensen *et al.* (eds.) *Levende Ord. Græsk, Latin, Oldtidskundskab*, Vejle: Klassikerforeningens kildehæfter, pp. 15–20.

Glamann, K. (1976) *Carlsbergfondet*, Copenhagen: Rhodos.

Goff, B. (ed.) (2005) *Classics and Colonialism*, London: Duckworth.

Goldhill, S. (2004) *Love, Sex and Tragedy: Why Classics Matters*, London: John Murray.

Goldhill, S. (2011) *Victorian Culture and Classical Antiquity: Art, Opera, Fiction and the Proclamation of Modernity*, Princeton: Princeton University Press.

Gropplero di Troppenburg, E. (1980) 'Die Innenausstattung der Glyptothek durch Leo v. Klenze', in K. Vierneisel and G. Leinz (eds.) *Glyptothek München 1830–1980*, Munchen: Prestel-Verlag, pp. 190–213.

Gruben, G. (2000) 'Klassische Bauforschung', in A.H. Borbein, T. Hölscher and P. Zanker (eds.) *Klassische Archäologie*, Berlin: Dietrich Reimer Verlag, pp. 251–279.

Grundtvig, N.F.S. (1848) 'Den Danske Høiskole, den Latinske Minister og Rigsdagsmanden fra Præstø', *Danskeren. Et ugeblad* 40, 3. kvartal, 20 December, 625–640.

Guldager, P. (1993) 'Antikmuseet, Aarhus Universitet', *Meddelelser fra Klassikerforeningen* 149, 13–20.

Hall, E. (2008) 'Putting the Class into Classical Reception', in L. Hardwick and C. Stray (eds.) *A Companion to Classical Receptions*, Oxford: Blackwell Publishing, pp. 386–397.

Hall, J.A., O. Korsgaard and O.K. Petersen (eds.) (2015) *Building the Nation: N.F.S. Grundtvig and Danish National Identity*, Montreal: McGill-Queens University Press.

Hamilakis, Y. (2007) *The Nation and Its Ruins: Antiquity, Archaeology, and National Imagination in Greece*, Oxford: Oxford University Press.

Hamilakis, Y. (2013) 'Double Colonization: The Story of the Excavations of the Athenian Agora (1924–1931)', *Hesperia* 82, 153–177.

Hamilakis, Y. (2016) 'Some Debts Can Never Be Repaid: The Archaeo-Politics of the Crisis', *Journal of Modern Greek Studies* 34.2, 227–264.

Hanink, J. (2017) *The Classical Debt: Greek Antiquity in an Era of Austerity*, Cambridge, MA: The Belknap Press of Harvard University Press.

Hansen, A.H. (2016) *Niebuhrs Museum. Souvenirs og sjældenheder indsamlet under Den Arabiske Rejse 1761–1767*, Copenhagen: Nationalmuseet.

Hansen, L. (2001) 'Historie, identitet og det danske europadilemma', *Den jyske historiker* 93, 113–131.

Hansen, L. (2002) 'Sustaining Sovereignty" The Danish Approach to Europe', in L. Hansen and O. Væver (eds.) *European Integration and National Identity: The Challenge of the Nordic States*, London and New York: Routledge, pp. 50–87.

Hansen, M.H. (1985) 'Dimensionsfaget oldtidskundskab', in H. Bolt-Jørgensen *et al.* (eds.) *Her kan vi se vores egne Vinduer – humaniora i gymnasiet*. Hjørring: Klassikerforeningens kildehæfter, pp. 91–94.

Harrison, R. (2013) *Heritage: Critical Approaches*, London: Routledge.

Hardwick, L. (2003) *Reception Studies*, Oxford: Oxford University Press.

Hardwick, L. and C. Stray (eds.) (2008) *A Companion to Classical Receptions*, Oxford: Blackwell Publishing.

Harloe, K. (2013) *Winckelmann and the Invention of Antiquity*, Oxford: Oxford University Press.

Hastrup, T. (1947) 'Oldtidskundskab', *Gymnasieskolen* 30, 14, 377–381.

Haue, H. (2003) *Almendannelse som ledestjerne. En undersøgelse af almendannelsens funktion i dansk gymnasieundervisning 1775–2000*, Odense: Syddansk Universitetsforlag.

Hauge, H. (2003) 'Globalisering er oldtidskundskab', in B. Andreasen (ed.) *Om fortidens fremtid – Forsvarstaler for det klassiske*, Aarhus: Aarhus Universitetsforlag, pp. 283–298.

Heiberg, J. (1889) *Græskens fremtidige stilling i skolen*, København: Det philologisk-historiske Samfund.

Hein, J. (2001) 'Repræsentation eller belæring?', *Nordisk Museologi* 2001.1–2, 153–170.

Held, D.t.D. (2000) 'Hellenism, Nationalism and the Ideology of Research in Humboldt's University', *Paper from the 19th International Congress on Historical Science*, Oslo. Online: www.oslo2000.uio.no/AIO/AIO16/group%204/Held.pdf (accessed 29 April 2018).

Hermansen, V. (1951) 'Fra Kunstkammer til Antik-Cabinet', in *Antik-Cabinettet 1851*, Copenhagen: The National Museum, pp. 9–56.

Hjorth, P.L. (1972) 'Nabosprogene i den højere danske skole. Et historisk rids med kommentarer', *Sprog i Norden*, Dansk Sprognævn, Copenhagen, pp. 25–43.

Høeg, S. (2003) 'Den græsk-romerske kulturs placering i Europa', in B. Andreasen (ed.) *Om fortidens fremtid – Forsvarstaler for det klassiske*, Aarhus: Aarhus Universitetsforlag, pp. 13–27.

Hoepfner, W. (2013) *Halikarnassos und das Maussolleion*, Mainz am Rhein: Philipp von Zabern.

Højlund, F. (1999) *Glob og paradisets have*, Højbjerg: Moesgård Museum.

Holtorf, C. (2007) *Archaeology Is a Brand! The Meaning of Archaeology in Contemporary Popular Culture*, Oxford: Archaeopress.

Horster, C. and L.M.A. Funder (eds.) (2017) *Antikkens veje til renæssancens Danmark*, Aarhus: Aarhus University Press.

Human, H. (2015) 'Democratising World Heritage: The Policies and Practices of Community Involvement in Turkey', *Journal of Social Archaeology* 15.2, 160–183.

Hvidberg-Hansen, G. and G. Oelsner (eds.) (2011) *The Spirit of Vitalism: Health, Beauty and Strength in Danish Art, 1890–1940*, Copenhagen: Museum Tusculanum Press.

Isager, S. and P. Pedersen (eds.) (2004) *The Salmakis Inscription and Hellenistic Halikarnassos* (Halikarnassian Studies IV), Odense: University Press of Southern Denmark.

Iuul, C. (1985) 'Klassikerforeningen 1935–1985 – en skizze', *Klassikerforeningens Meddelelser* 100, 18–25.

Jacobaeus, H. (1696) *Museum Regium*, Copenhagen: Joachim Schmetgen.

Jacobsen, C. (1906) *Ny Carlsberg Glyptoteks Tilblivelse*, Copenhagen: Ny Carlsberg Glyptotek.

Jakobsen, T.B. (2010) 'Oldsagskommissionens tidlige år, forudsætninger og internationale forbindelser', in *Annual of the Royal Society of Northern Antiquaries 2007*, Copenhagen: Det Kongelige Nordiske Oldskriftsselskab, pp. 161–192.

Jansen, F.J.B. (1985) 'Når oldtid bliver til nutid', in H. Bolt-Jørgensen *et al.* (eds.) *Her kan vi se vores egne Vinduer – humaniora i gymnasiet*, Hjørring: Klassikerforeningens kildehæfter, pp. 51–56.

Jenkins, I. (1992) *Archaeologists and Aesthetes in the Sculpture Galleries of the British Museum 1800–1939*, London: British Museum Press.

Jenkins, I. and G.F. Waywell (eds.) (1997) *Sculptors and Sculpture of Caria and the Dodecanese*, London: British Museum Press.

Jensen, B.E. (2008) *Kulturarv – et identitetspolitisk konfliktfelt*, København: Gads forlag.

Jensen, J. (1992) *Thomsens Museum – Historien om Nationalmuseet*, Copenhagen: Gyldendal.

Jeppesen, K. (1958) *Paradeigmata: Three Mid-Fourth Century Main Works of Hellenistic Architecture*, Aarhus: Jutland Archaeological Society Publications.

Jeppesen, K. (1976) 'Neue Ergebnisse zur Wiederherstullung des Maussolleions von Halikarnassos. 4. Vorläufiger Bericht der dänischen Halikarnassosexpedition', *Istanbuler Mitteilungen* 26, 47–99.

Jeppesen, K. (1987) *The Theory of the Alternative Erechtheion: Premises, Definition, and Implications*, Aarhus: Aarhus University Press.

Jeppesen, K. (1989) *Ikaros: The Hellenistic Settlements, Vol. 3: The Sacred Enclosure in the Early Hellenistic Period*, Aarhus: Aarhus University Press.

Jeppesen, K. (1992) 'Tot operum opus. Ergebnisse der dänischen Forschungen zum Maussolleion von Halikarnass seit 1966', *Jahrbuch des deutschen archäologischen Instituts* 107, 59–102.

Jeppesen, K. (1999) 'Et klassisk verdensvidunder til revision. Mausollæet i Halikarnassos', in P. Guldager Bilde, V. Nørskov and P. Pedersen (eds.) *Hvad fandt vi? En gravedagbog fra Institut for Klassisk Arkæologi, Aarhus Universitet*, Aarhus: Tidsskriftet Sfinx, pp. 39–56.

Jeppesen, K. (2007) 'A Fresh Approach to the Problems of the Parthenon Frieze', *Proceedings of the Danish Institute at Athens* 5, 101–172.

Jeppesen, K. (2011) 'Appendix 1: Labraunda Revisited', in L. Karlsson and S. Carlsson (eds.) *Labraunda and Karia: Proceedings of the International Symposium Commemorating Sixty Years of Swedish Archaeological Work in Labraunda*, Uppsala: Uppsala Universitet, pp. 463–470.

Jezernik, B. (2007) 'Constructing Identities on Marbles and Terracotta: Representations of Classical Heritage in Greece and Turkey', *Museum Anthropology* 30.1, 3–20.

Johansen, K.F. (1943) 'Klassisk arkæologi', in S. Dahl (ed.) *Danmarks Kultur ved Aar 1940, bind 7. Den videnskabelige Kultur*, Copenhagen: Det danske Forlag, pp. 165–174.

Johansen, F. (1985a) 'Oldtidskundskab – nu sættes den i kælderen', in H. Bolt-Jørgensen *et al.* (eds.) *Her kan vi se vores egne Vinduer – humaniora i gymnasiet*, Hjørring: Klassikerforeningens kildehæfter, pp. 41–45.

Johansen, F. (1985b) 'Oldtidskundskab og filolosofi', in H. Bolt-Jørgensen *et al.* (eds.) *Her kan vi se vores egne Vinduer – humaniora i gymnasiet*, Hjørring: Klassikerforeningens kildehæfter, pp. 23–30.

Jonas, U. (2014) 'On the Church, the State, and the School: Grundtvig as Enlightenment Philosopher and Social Thinker', in J.A. Hall, O. Korsgaard and O.K. Petersen (eds.) (2015) *Building the Nation: N.F.S. Grundtvig and Danish National Identity*, Montreal: McGill-Queens University Press, pp. 170–191.

Jørgensen, C.M. (2005) 'Civilisation og nation i dansk dannelsestænkning i det nittende århundrede', in P.F. Bang (ed.) *Fremmed og moderne*, Aarhus: Aarhus Universitetsforlag, pp. 97–112.

Jørgensen, K.B., L. Ipsen, R. Stobbe, C. Dahl and C. Neutsky-Wulff (2014) *Perspektivering i oldtidskundskab – lødighed og væsentlighed i tekstvalg*. Online: www.klassikerforeningen.dk/wp-content/uploads/Old-perspektivtekster-2012.pdf (accessed 22 June 2018).

Jørgensen, L.B. and D. Porphyrios (1987) *Neoclassical Architecture in Copenhagen and Athens*, London: Architectural Design.

Joshel, S.R., M. Malamud and D.T. McGuire, Jr. (eds.) (2001) *Imperial Projections: Ancient Rome in Modern Popular Culture*, Baltimore: Johns Hopkins University Press.

Kaarstad, T. (1985) 'Humaniora', in H. Bolt-Jørgensen *et al.* (eds.) *Her kan vi se vores egne Vinduer – humaniora i gymnasiet*, Hjørring: Klassikerforeningens kildehæfter, pp. 45–47.

Kassebeer, S. (2017) 'Kulturministeren: "Der bliver simpelthen læst for lidt Platon i dag"', *Berlingske Tidende* 19 November. Online: www.b.dk/kultur/kulturministeren-der-bliver-simpelthen-laest-for-lidt-platon-i-dag (accessed 25 June 2018).

Kirke-og Undervisningsministeriet (1889) *Forhandlinger om en Reform af Undervisningen i de lærde Skoler*, Copenhagen: Kirke-og Undervisningsministeriet.

Kjeldbæk, E. (2012) 'Europe Meets the World: An Overview', in L.K. Christensen, P. Grinder-Hansen, E. Kjelbæk and B.B. Rasmussen (eds.) *Europe Meets the World*, Copenhagen: The National Museum, pp. 416–451.

Knell, S. (2011) 'National Museums and the National Imagination', in S. Knell, P. Aronson, and A.B. Amundsen (eds.) *National Museums: New Studies from around the World*, London: Routledge, pp. 3–28.

Kockel, V. (1993) 'Rom über die Alpen tragen. Korkmodelle antiker Architektur im 18. und 19. Jahrhundert', in W. Helmberger and V. Kockel (eds.) *Rom über die Alpen tragen. Fürsten sammeln antike Architektur. Die Aschaffenburger Korkmodelle*, Landshut/Ergolding, Arcos Verlag, pp. 11–32.

Kockel, V. (1998) *Phelloplastica. Modelli in sughero dell'architettura antica nel XVIII secolo nella collezione di Gustavo III di Svezia*, Jonsered: Paul Åströms forlag.

Kohl, P.L., M. Kozelsky and N. Ben-Yehuda (eds.) (2007) *Selective Remembrances: Archaeology in the Construction, Commemoration, and Consecration of National Pasts*, Chicago: The University of Chicago Press.

Krarup, P. (1953) 'Greek Culture in Danish Schools', *Greece and Rome* 22.64, 11–17.

Krischen, F. (1956) *Weltwunder der Baukunst in Babylonien und Jonien*, Tübingen: Verlag Ernst Wasmuth.

Krogh, L. and P. Guldager Bilde (1997) *Pegasus og Tanagra. Antikken i J.F. Willumsens kunst og samling*, Frederiksund: J.F. Willumsens Museum.

Kryger, K. (1991) 'Dansk identitet i nyklassicistisk kunst. Nationale tendenser og nationalt særpræg 1750–1800', in O. Feldbæk (ed.) *Dansk Identitetshistorie, Vol. 1: Fædreland og modersmål 1536–1789*, Copenhagen: Reitzels Forlag, pp. 231–418.

Kulturministeriet (2003) *Udredning om Bevaring af Kulturarven*, Copenhagen: Kulturministeriet.

Larsen, C. and J.E. Larsen (2011) 'Between "Freight-Shippers" and Nordists: The Political Implications of Educational Historiography in Denmark', *Jahrbuch für historische Bildungsforschung* 17, 245–269.

Larsen, C., E. Nørr and P. Sonne (2013) *Da skolen tog form 1780–1850. Dansk skolehistorie bind 2*, Aarhus: Aarhus Universitetsforlag.

Larsen, J.E. (2006) *J.N. Madvigs dannelsestanker*, Copenhagen: Museum Tusculanum Press.

Liventhal, V. (1986) 'C.T. Falbe – søofficer og arkæolog. En dansk mandsskæbne fra det forrige århundrede', *Museum Tusculanum* 56, 337–361.

Lowenthal, D. (1985) *The Past Is a Foreign Country*, Cambridge: Cambridge University Press.

Lund, J. and B.B. Rasmussen (1995) *Greeks, Etruscans, Romans: The Collection of Antiquities*, Copenhagen: The National Museum.

Lundgreen-Nielsen, F. (1993) 'Kampen om Rom. Romerriget i dansk litteratur 1750–1900', in O.S. Due and J. Isager (red.) *Imperium Romanum. Realitet, ide, ideal, bind III*, Aarhus: Tidsskriftet Sfinx, pp. 259–298.

Lynning, K.H. (2007) 'Dannelse og naturvidenskab i den lærde skole 1878–1886', *Slagmark* 7, 50–65.

Macdonald, S. (2013) *Memorylands: Heritage and Identity in Europe Today*, Abingdon and New York: Routledge.

Madvig, J.N. (1887) *Livserindringer*, Copenhagen: Gyldendalske Boghandels Forlag.

Malpas, J. (2012) *Heidegger and the Thinking of Place: Explorations in the Topology of Being*, Cambridge, MA: The MIT Press.

Malpas, J. (2014) 'Thinking Topographically: Place, Space, and Geography', Online: www.academia.edu/4185517/Thinking_Topographically_Place_Space_and_ Geography (accessed 13 June 2018).

Mansur, F. (1972) *Bodrum: A Town in the Aegean*, Leiden: Brill.

Mansur, F. (1999) *Bodrum. Dün-Bugün*, Istanbul: Ana Yayıncılik.

Marchand, S.L. (1996) *Down from Olympus: Archaeology and Philhellenism in Germany, 1750–1970*, Princeton, NJ: Princeton University Press.

Marlowe, E. (2013) *Shaky Ground: Context, Connoisseurship and the History of Roman Art*, London: Bloomsbury.

Martindale, C. (2006) 'Thinking through Reception', in C. Martindale and R.F. Thomas (eds.) *Classics and the Uses of Reception*, Oxford: Blackwell Publishing, pp. 1–13.

Martindale, C. (2007) 'Reception', in C.W. Kallendorf (ed.) *A Companion to the Classical Tradition*, Oxford: Blackwell Publishing, pp. 297–311.

Martindale, C. (2013) 'Reception: A New Humanism? Receptivity, Pedagogy and the Transhistorical', *Classical Receptions Journal* 5.2, 169–183.

Martinez, J.-L. (2011) 'Les salles d'art grec classique et hellénistique du musée du Louvre', *Revue Du Louvre* 1.1, 32–42.

Maussolleion 1 = Jeppesen, K., F. Højlund and K. Aaris-Sørensen (1981) *The Maussolleion at Halikarnassos: Reports of the Danish Archaeological Expedition to Bodrum, Vol, 1: The Sacrificial Deposit*, Aarhus: Jutland Archaeological Society Publications.

Maussolleion 2 = Jeppesen, K. and A. Luttrell (1986) *The Maussolleion at Halikarnassos. Reports of the Danish Archaeological Expedition to Bodrum, Vol. 2: The Written Sources and Their Archaeological Background*, Aarhus: Jutland Archaeological Society Publications.

Maussolleion 3 = Pedersen, P. (1991) *The Maussolleion at Halikarnassos: Reports of the Danish Archaeological Expedition to Bodrum, Vol. 3:1 and 3:2: The Maussolleion Terrace and Accessory Structures*, Aarhus: Aarhus University Press.

Maussolleion 4 = Jeppesen, K. (2000) *The Maussolleion at Halikarnassos: Reports of the Danish Archaeological Expedition to Bodrum, Vol. 4: The Quadrangle: The Foundations of the Maussolleion and Its Sepulchral Compartments*, Aarhus: Aarhus University Press.

Maussolleion 5 = Jeppesen, K. (2002) *The Maussolleion at Halikarnassos: Reports of the Danish Archaeological Expedition to Bodrum, Vol. 5: The Superstructure:*

A Comparative Analysis of the Architectural, Sculptural, and Literary Evidence, Aarhus: Aarhus University Press.

Mausolleion 6 = Zahle, J. and K. Kjeldsen (2004) *The Maussolleion at Halikarnassos: Reports of the Danish Archaeological Expedition, Vol. 6: Subterranean and Pre-Maussollan Structures on the Site of the Maussolleion: The Finds from the Tomb Chamber of the Maussollos*, Aarhus: Aarhus University Press.

Mausolleion 7 = Vaag, L.E., V. Nørskov and J. Lund (2002) *The Maussolleion at Halikarnassos: Reports of the Danish Archaeological Expedition to Bodrum, Vol. 7: The Pottery: Ceramic Material and Other Finds from Selected Contexts*, Aarhus: Aarhus University Press.

McElduff, S. (2006) 'Fractured Understandings: Towards a History of Classical Reception among Non-Elite Groups', in C. Martindale and R.F. Thomas (eds.) *Classics and the Uses of Reception*, Oxford: Blackwell Publishing, pp. 180–191.

Meier, C. (2011) *A Culture of Freedom: Ancient Greece and the Origins of Europe*, Oxford: Oxford University Press.

Mejer, J. (2003) 'International kultur og international sprog', in H. Bolt-Jørgensen *et al.* (eds.) *Levende Ord. Græsk, Latin, Oldtidskundskab*, Vejle: Klassikerforeningens kildehæfter, pp. 79–82.

Melander, T. (1993) *Thorvaldsens Antikker – en temmelig udvalgt samling*, Copenhagen: Thorvaldsens Museum.

Mentz, S. (2004) 'Forestillede fællesskaber. En kommentar til Benedict Andersons nationalitetsteorier i dansk og international sammenhæng', *Fortid og Nutid*, 50–54.

Meskell, L. (2000) 'The Practice and Politics of Archaeology in Egypt', *Annals of the New York Academy of Sciences* 925.1, 146–169.

Meskell, L. (2005) 'Sites of Violence: Terrorism, Tourism, and Heritage in the Archaeological Present', in L. Meskell and P. Pels (eds.) *Embedding Ethics*, Oxford: Berg, pp. 123–146.

Miles, L. and A. Wivel (eds.) (2014) *Denmark and the European Union*, London: Routledge.

Miller, P.N. (2017) *History and Its Objects: Antiquarianism and Material Culture since 1500*, Ithaca: Cornell University Press.

Ministerielt cirkulære angående undervisningen i gymnasiet med udkast til anordning om studentereksamen 1906, 4.12, nr. 367. Online: http://library.au.dk/uploads/tx_lfskolelov/Cir._af_4._dec._1906._Nr_367.pdf (accessed 22 June 2018).

Moltesen, M. (2006a) 'Carl Jacobsen og hans antiksamling', *Meddelelser fra Ny Carlsberg Glyptotek* 8, 27–38.

Moltesen, M. (2006b) 'Carl Jacobsen som antiksamler – imod middelmådighed', *Meddelelser fra Ny Carlsberg Glyptotek* 8, 39–53.

Moltesen, M. (2012) *Perfect Partners: The Collaboration between Carl Jacobsen and His Agent in Rome Wolfgang Helbig in the Formation of the Ny Carlsberg Glyptotek 1887–1914*, Copenhagen: Ny Carlsberg Glyptotek.

Moltesen, M. and J.S. Østergaard (2006) 'Kunst, kronologi og kontekst. Nyopstillingen af Glyptotekets antikke skulpturer 2006', in F. Friborg and A.M. Nielsen (eds.) *Ny Carlsberg Glyptotek i Tiden*, Copenhagen: Ny Carlsberg Glyptotek, pp. 205–214.

Mortensen, E. and B. Poulsen (eds.) (2016) *Death and Burial in Karia* (Halicarnassian Studies VI), Odense: University Press of Southern Denmark.

Müller, S. (1907) *Nationalmuseet hundrede Aar efter Grundlæggelsen*, Copenhagen: The National Museum.

Nelis, J. (2008) 'Modernist Neo-Classicism and Antiquity in the Political Religion of Nazism: Adolf Hitler as Poietes of the Third Reich', *Totalitarian Movements and Political Religions* 9.4, 475–490.

Newton, C.T. (1862) *A History of Discoveries at Halicarnassos, Cnidus and Branchidæ*, London: Day and Son.

Nielsen, A.M. and F. Johansen (1996) *Hovedværker i Ny Carlsberg Glyptotek*, Copenhagen: Ny Carlsberg Glyptotek.

Nielsen, M. (ed.) (1990) *The Classical Heritage in Nordic Art and Architecture: Acts of the Seminar Held at the University of Copenhagen, 1st-3rd November 1988*, Copenhagen: Museum Tusculanum Press.

Nielsen, M. and A. Rathje (eds.) (2010) *Johannes Wiedewelt: A Danish Artist in the Search of the Past, Shaping the Future* (Acta Hyperborea 11), Copenhagen: Museum Tusculanum Press.

Nielsen, V. (1912) *Den græske litteraturs historie. En oversigt til brug ved undervisning i oldtidskundskab*, Copenhagen: Johs. Marchkers Boghandel.

Niklasson, E. and H. Hølleland (2018) 'The Scandinavian Far-Right and the New Politicisation of Heritage', *Journal of Social Archaeology* 18.2, 121–148.

Nørregård-Nielsen, H.E. (2004) 'A Dynasty of Brewers and Collectors', in *Ancient Art to Post-Impressionism: Masterpieces from the Ny Carlsberg Glyptotek, Copenhagen*, London: Thames and Hudson, pp. 10–13.

Norris, M. (2016) *A Pilgrimage to the Past* (Ugglan: Lund Studies in the History of Ideas and Sciences, Minerva Series 19), Lund: Media Tryck.

Nørskov, V. (2002) *Greek Vases in New Contexts: An Aspect of the Reception of Antiquity*, Aarhus: Aarhus University Press.

Nørskov, V. (ed.) (2008) *Antikken i Århus*, Aarhus: Antikmuseet.

Nørskov, V. and T.M. Kristensen (forthcoming) 'Imagined Geography: Classical Antiquity in Danish Education and Heritage', in L. Galani, E. Mavrikaki and K. Skourdoulis (eds.) *Geographical Literacy and European Heritage: A Challenging Convention in the Field of Education*, Limassol: Solva-tech.

Nyholm, P. (1999) 'Underværket i Bodrum', *Jyllands-Posten* 21 February, Ferie & Fritid, 1–2.

Olesen, M.N. (2010) 'Bildung: Then and Now in Danish High School and University Teaching and How to Integrate Bildung into Modern University Teaching', *Forum on Public Policy* 2, 1–23.

Østergaard, J.S. (2011) '*Semper Ardens:* Facaden af Hack Kampmanns bygning til Glyptotekets antikke samling', in *Festskrift til Chr. Gorm Tortzen* (AIGIS Supplementum I). Online: http://aigis.igl.ku.dk/aigis/CGT/Jan_Stubbe.pdf (accessed 22 June 2018).

Østergaard, U. (1992) 'Peasants and Danes. The Danish National Identity and Political Culture', *Comparative Studies in Society and History* 34.1, 3–27.

Østergaard, U. (2004) 'The Danish Path to Modernity', *Thesis Eleven* 77.1, 25–43.

Özdoğan, M. (1998) 'Ideology and Archaeology in Turkey', in L. Meskell (ed.) *Archaeology Under Fire: Nationalism, Politics and Heritage in the Eastern Mediterranean and Near East*, London: Routledge, pp. 111–123.

Pade, M. (2003) 'Shakespeare og Plutarch', in B. Andreasen (ed.) *Om fortidens fremtid – Forsvarstaler for det klassiske*, Aarhus: Aarhus Universitetsforlag, pp. 59–75.

Panourgiá, N. (2004) 'Colonizing the ideal', *Aneglaki: Journal of the Theoretical Humanities* 9.2, 165–180.

Pasquier, A., S. Descamps and M. Denoyelle (1997) 'Le département des Antiquités grecques, étrusques et romaines: agrandissement et nouvelles presentations', *Revue Du Louvre* 47, 29–38.

Paul, J. (2010) 'Cinematic Receptions of Antiquity: The Current State of Play', *Classical Receptions Journal* 2.1, 136–155.

Paul, J. (2013) *Film and the Classical Epic Tradition*, Oxford: Oxford University Press.

Pedersen, C.S. (2007) 'Glyptoteket vil pirke til Os og de Andre', *Politiken* 23 October.

Pedersen, P. (1994) 'The Ionian Renaissance and Some Aspects of the Its Origin within the Field of Architecture and Planning', in J. Isager (ed.) *Hekatomnid Caria and the Ionian Renaissance: Acts of the International Symposium at the Department of Greek and Roman Studies, Odense University, 28–29 November, 1991* (Halicarnassian Studies I), Odense: Odense University Press, pp. 11–35.

Pedersen, P. (1999a) '"Byen ligner et teater": En romersk arkitekt i Halikarnassos', in P. Guldager Bilde, V. Nørskov and P. Pedersen (eds.) *Hvad fandt vi? En gravedagbog fra Institut for Klassisk Arkæologi, Aarhus Universitet*, Aarhus: Tidsskriftet Sfinx, pp. 57–68.

Pedersen, P. (1999b) 'Byarkæologi. Jagten på Kong Maussollos' forsvundne hovedstad', in P. Guldager Bilde, V. Nørskov and P. Pedersen (eds.) *Hvad fandt vi? En gravedagbog fra Institut for Klassisk Arkæologi, Aarhus Universitet*, Aarhus: Tidsskriftet Sfinx, pp. 69–79.

Pedersen, P. (2009) 'The Palace of Maussollos in Halikarnassos and Some Thoughts on Its Karian and International Context', in F. Rumscheid (ed.) *Die Karer und die Anderen. Internationales Kolloquium an der Freien Universität Berlin 13. bis 15. Oktober 2005*, Bonn: Habelt, pp. 315–348.

Pelt, M. (2000) 'Vi er alle sammen grækere. Den europæiske filhellenisme fra passion og politik til pædagogisk projekt', in J. Christiansen and A.M. Nielsen (eds.) *København-Athen tur/retur. Danmark og Grækenland i 1800-tallet*, København: Ny Carlsberg Glyptotek, pp. 31–42.

Petersen, E. (1985) 'Om kilder og vandbærere', in H. Bolt-Jørgensen *et al.* (eds.) *Her kan vi se vores egne Vinduer – humaniora i gymnasiet*, Hjørring: Klassikerforeningens kildehæfter, pp. 71–75.

Prettejohn, E. (2006) 'Reception and Ancient Art: The Case of Venus de Milo', in C. Martindale and R.F. Thomans (eds.) *Classics and the Uses of Reception*, Oxford: Blackwell Publishing, pp. 227–249.

Prettejohn, E. (2012) *The Modernity of Ancient Sculpture: Greek Sculpture and Modern Art from Winckelmann to Picasso*, London: I.B. Tauris.

Poulsen, B. (2011) 'Halikarnassos during the Imperiod Period and Late Antiquity', in L. Karlsson and S. Carlsson (eds.) *Labraunda and Karia: Proceedings of the International Symposium commemorating Sixty Years of Swedish Archaeological Work in Labraunda*, Uppsala: Uppsala Universitet, pp. 424–443.

Raabyemagle, H. and C.M. Smidt (eds.) (1998) *Klassicisme i København. Arkitekturen på C.F. Hansens tid*, Copenhagen: Gyldendal.

Rasmussen, B.B. (1995) 'En rejse omkring Middelhavet: den ny antiksamling på Nationalmuseet', *Nationalmuseets Arbejdsmark*, 89–100.

Rasmussen, B.B., J.S. Jensen and J. Lund (2000) *Christian VIII and the National Museum*, Copenhagen: The National Museum.

Rasmussen, B.B., J.S. Jensen, J. Lund and M. Märcher (2008) *Peter Oluf Brøndsted (1780–1842): A Danish Classicist in His European Context* (Historisk-filosofiske tekster 31), Copenhagen: The Royal Danish Academy of Sciences and Letters.

Rasmussen, B.B. and J. Lund (2012) 'The Story Begins', in L.K. Christensen, P. Grinder-Hansen, E. Kjelbæk and B.B. Rasmussen (eds.) *Europe Meets the World*, Copenhagen: The National Museum, pp. 32–65.

Rasmussen, B.B., J. Lund, H.W. Horsnæs, W. Helle, P. Pentz and A.H. Hansen (2012) 'Superpower', in L.K. Christensen, P. Grinder-Hansen, E. Kjeldbæk and B.B. Rasmussen (eds.) *Europe Meets the World*, Copenhagen: The National Museum, pp. 66–115.

Rathje, A. and J. Lund (1991) 'Danes Overseas: A Short History of Danish Classical Archaeological Fieldwork', in T. Fischer-Hansen, P. Guldager, J. Lund, M. Nielsen and A. Rathje (eds.) *Recent Danish Research in Classical Archaeology: Tradition and Renewal*, Copenhagen: Museum Tusculanum Press, pp. 11–56.

Rerup, L. (1993) 'The Impact on Grundtvig on Early Danish nationalism', *History of European Ideas* 16, 323–330.

Riis, P.J. (1979) 'Klassisk og nærorientalsk arkæologi', in P.J. Jensen (ed.) *Københavns Universitet 1479–1979. Bind XI. Det filosofiske fakultet, 4. del*, Copenhagen: G.E.C. Gads Forlag, pp. 121–160.

Said, E.W. (1978) *Orientalism*, London: Routledge.

Scharling, C.H. (1903) *Den lærde Skole og Universitetet: et Indlæg i Skolesagen*, Copenhagen: Gads Folag.

Schepelern, H.D. (1985) 'Tradition og traditioner i gymnasiets klassiske fag', in H. Bolt-Jørgensen *et al.* (eds.) *Her kan vi se vores egne Vinduer – humaniora i gymnasiet*, Hjørring: Klassikerforeningens kildehæfter, pp. 56–63.

Scott, M. (2014) *Delphi: A History of the Center of the Ancient World*, Princeton: Princeton University Press.

Settis, S. (2006) *The Future of the Classical*, Cambridge and Malden: Polity.

Shanks, M. (1996) *Classical Archaeology of Greece: Experiences of the Discipline*, London: Routledge.

Siapkas, J. (2017) *Från Laokoon till Troja* (Antikvetenskapens teoretiska landskap 1), Lund: Nordic Academic Press.

Siapkas, J. and L. Sjögren (2014) *Displaying the Ideals of Antiquity: The Petrified Gaze*, London: Routledge.

Silk, M., I. Gildenhard and R. Barrow (2014) *The Classical Tradition: Art, Literature, Thought*, Malden, MA: Wiley Blackwell.

Skovgaard-Petersen, V. (1976) *Dannelse og demokrati. Fra latin-til almenskole. Lov om højere almenskoler 24. april 1903*, Copenhagen: Gyldendal.

Sløk, J. (1985) 'Det knuste spejl', in H. Bolt-Jørgensen *et al.* (eds.) *Her kan vi se vores egne Vinduer – humaniora i gymnasiet*, Hjørring: Klassikerforeningens kildehæfter, pp. 15–18.

Smith, A.D. (1998) *Nationalism and Modernism: A Critical Survey of Recent Theories of Nations and Nationalism*, London: Taylor and Francis.

Smith, L. (2006) *Uses of Heritage*, London: Routledge.

Sommer, A.-L. (ed.) (2009) *Den Danske Arkitektur*, Copenhagen: Gyldendal.

Søndergaard, S. (2006) 'Statuemani', *Meddelelser fra Ny Carlsberg Glyptotek 8*, 15–26.

Sortkær, A. (2008) 'Hvilken fortræffelig gave fra den danske nation til videnskaben! Fremkomsten af internationale videnskabelige ekspeditioner i 1700-tallet', *Den jyske historiker* 119, 5–25.

Squire, M. (2012) 'Classical Archaeology and the Contexts of Art History', in R. Osborne and S. Alcock (eds.) *Classical Archaeology*, Oxford: Wiley-Blackwell, pp. 468–500.

Stavnem, R. (2011) 'Odin og Tor i Troja – mytologi, historie og allegori i Snorris Edda', in O. Høiris and B. Poulsen (eds.) *Antikkens Verden*, Aarhus: Aarhus University Press, pp. 457–468.

Stx-bekendtgørelsen (2004) 'Bekendtgørelse om uddannelsen til studentereksamen, BEK rn. 1348 af 15/12/2004', Online: www.retsinformation.dk/forms/R0710. aspx?id=24699 (accessed 15 January 2018).

Stx-læreplaner (2017) 'C, stx: Vejledning. Undervisningsministeriet Styrelsen for Undervisning og Kvalitet Gymnasie-og Tilsynskontoret, august 2017', Online: https://uvm.dk/gymnasiale-uddannelser/fag-og-laereplaner/laereplaner-2017/stx-laereplaner-2017 (accessed 15 January 2018).

Tamm, D. (2003) 'Antikrapporten og dens anbefalinger', in H. Bolt-Jørgensen, I. Gjørup, S. Høeg, F. Jordsalg, K.F. Staugaard and C.G Tortzen (eds.) *Levende ord. Græsk, latin og oldtidskundskab*, Hjørring: Klassikerforeningens kildehæfter, pp. 65–69.

Thomsen, O. (2003) 'Logoslandet', in B. Andreasen (ed.) *Om fortidens fremtid – Forsvarstaler for det klassiske*, Aarhus: Aarhus Universitetsforlag, pp. 116–135.

Thomsen, O. (2005) 'Indledning', in *Samtiden anbefalet. En antologi til undervisning i oldtidskundskab*, Aarhus: Klassikerforeningens kildehæfter, pp. 9–17.

Thonemann, P. (2018) 'Review of Philipp Niewöhner (ed.)', *The Archaeology of Byzantine Anatolia* (Oxford 2017)', *Antiquity* 92.361, 261–262.

Tortzen, G. (2003) 'Videnskabshistorien og de klassiske fag', in B. Andreasen (ed.) *Om fotidens fremtid – Forsvarstaler for det klassiske*, Aarhus: Aarhus Universitetsforlag, pp. 227–240.

Tsigakou, F.-M. (1981) *The Rediscovery of Greece: Travellers and Painters in the Romantic Era*, London: Thames and Hudson.

Undervisningsministeriet (1988) *Oldtidskundskab 1988. Bekendtgørelse og vejledende retningslinjer*, Copenhagen: Undervisningsministeriet.

Undervisningsministeriet (1997) *Uddannelsesredegørelse 1997*, Copenhagen: Undervisningsministeret.

Undervisningsministeriet (2010) *Oldtidskundskab C – Stx. Råd og vink.* Afdelingen for gymnasiale uddannelser. Online: www.uvm.dk/-/media/Filer/UVM/Udd/Gym/PDF10/Vejledninger%20til%20laereplaner/Stx/100629_vejl_oldtidsk undskab_C_stx.pdf&usg=AOvVaw0cuMAfxYhvo4Ck1v6vGK2q (accessed 22 June 2018).

Ussing, J.L. (1844) *De nominibus vasorum græcorum*, Copenhagen: Typis Blanci Luni.

Ussing, J.L. (1873) *Fra en Rejse, Archæologiske Skildringer*, Copenhagen: Gyldendalske Boghandel.

Ussing, J.L. (1882) *Fra Hellas og Lilleasien i Foraaret 1882*, Copenhagen: Gyldendalske Boghandels Forlag.

Ussing, J.L. (1897) *Pergamos. Dens Historie og Monumenter*, Copenhagen: Universitetsboghandler G.E.C. Gad.

Ussing, J.L. (1906) *Af mit Levned*, Copenhagen: Gyldendalske Boghandel Nordisk Forlag.

Vasunia, P. and S.A. Stephens (2010) 'Introduction', in P. Vasunia and S.A. Stephens (eds.) *Classics and National Cultures*, Oxford: Oxford University Press, pp. 1–15.

Vout, C. (2012) 'Putting the Art into Artefact', in R. Osborne and S. Alcock (eds.) *Classical Archaeology*, Oxford: Wiley-Blackwell, pp. 442–467.

Vuorela, M. and K.B. Fals (2016) 'Glyptoteket leverer stjålen skat tilbage', *Politiken* 5 July.

Wagner, P. (2003) 'Videnskabernes sprog', in H. Bolt-Jørgensen *et al.* (eds.) *Levende Ord. Græsk, Latin, Oldtidskundskab*, Vejle: Klassikerforeningens kildehæfter, pp. 35–39.

Walker, S. (2013) 'A "Democratic Turn" at the Ashmolean Museum', in L. Hardwick and S. Harrison (eds.) *Classics in the Modern World: A Democratic Turn?*, Oxford: Oxford University Press, pp. 394–408.

Weiss, R. (1969) *The Renaissance Discovery of Classical Antiquity*, London: B. Blackwell.

Whitehead, C. (2009) *Museums and the Construction of Disciplines: Art and Archaeology in Nineteenth-Century Britain*, London and New York: Bloomsbury Academic.

Whitehead, C., S. Eckersley, K. Lloyd, and R. Mason (eds.) (2015) *Museums, Migration and Identity in Europe: Peoples, Places and Identities*, London: Routledge.

Williams, R. (2013) *The Fisherman of Halicarnassus*, Ankara: Bilgi.

Windfeld, B. (1985) 'Bent Windfeld i samtale med Søren Hindsholm', in H. Bolt-Jørgensen *et al.* (eds.) *Her kan vi se vores egne Vinduer – humaniora i gymnasiet*, Hjørring: Klassikerforeningens kildehæfter, pp. 94–98.

Winkelmann, J.J. (1763) *Geschichte der Kunst des Alterthum*, Dresden: Walther.

Wintle, M. (2016) 'Islam as Europe's "Other" in the Long Term: Some Discontinuities', *History* 101.344, 42–61.

Wivel, P. (1985) 'Et rejsebrev fra Athen', in H. Bolt-Jørgensen *et al.* (eds.) *Her kan vi se vores egne Vinduer – humaniora i gymnasiet*, Hjørring: Klassikerforeningens kildehæfter, pp. 9–14.

Wolf, F.A. (1807) 'Darstellung der Alterthumswissenschaft', *Museum der Alterthumswissenschaft* 1, 1–145.

Wolf, F.A. (1818) *Omrids af oldtidsvidenskabens encyclopædie, oversat, med en indledning af P.O. Brøndsted*, Copenhagen: Andreas Seidelin.

Wulf-Jørgensen, I. (1985) 'Skarpretteren bukker for ofret', in H. Bolt-Jørgensen *et al.* (eds.) *Her kan vi se vores egne Vinduer – humaniora i gymnasiet*, Hjørring: Klassikerforeningens kildehæfter, pp. 67–70.

Yalouri, E. (2001) *The Acropolis: Global Fame, Local Claim*, Oxford: Berg.

Zahle, J. (2005) 'Afstøbningssamlinger i Danmark', in E.J. Bencard (ed.) *Afstøbningssamlingen – død eller levende?*, Hornbæk: Afstøbningssamlingens Venner, pp. 177–183.

Zeeberg, P. (2003) 'En stadig proces – latinske klassikere i oversættelse', in B. Andreasen (ed.) *Om fortidens fremtid – Forsvarstaler for det klassiske*, Aarhus: Aarhus Universitetsforlag, pp. 241–260.

Zibrandtsen, M. (2003) 'De gymnasiale metafag', *Politiken* 4 February.

Index

Aarhus Museum 50
Aarhus University 84, 99
Aischylos 30–33
Alexander the Great 55, 100–101
American School of Classical Studies
    at Athens 78
Anderson, Benedict 7
Antiquities Commission 14, 50–51
Aristotle 25, 30, 34, 37
art, Greek 39, 47, 57, 68; Roman 47
art history 47, 53, 57, 68, 70
Atatürk, Mustafa Kemal 85
Athens 1, 3, 8–9, 13, 18, 24, 33–34,
    37–38, 46, 48, 53, 55, 59, 71, 78–79,
    87, 93, 99; acropolis 1–2, 8, 10, 18,
    59, 100; Acropolis Museum 46
autopsia 26, 29, 33

Barroso, Jose Manuel 100
Bauforschung 84, 88–90, 93, 96
Bavaria 8
Berlin 23, 39, 45, 51
Bildung 14, 17, 23–25, 27, 34, 74, 102
Blinkenberg, Christian 81
Blüdnikow, Bent 101
Bock, Mette 4
Bodrum 17–18, 76–99
British Museum 9, 16, 45, 51,
    83–84, 88
Brøndsted, Peter Oluf 24–25, 79

Carlsberg Foundation 16, 61, 79–81, 85
Carstens, Anne Marie 96
Christian VIII (King of Denmark) 17,
    51, 58–60

classical archaeology 16, 18, 25, 47–48,
    53, 61, 68, 76, 78–80, 83–84, 97, 99
Classical Association 30, 33, 36
classical reception studies 4–5
Classical Studies *see Oldtidskundskab*
classicism, definition of 2
Cold War 1, 39
collecting 5, 16, 45–74, 79
colonies 3; Danish 12
Copenhagen 9, 12–13, 24–25, 30, 40,
    61–63, 66, 75, 103
Copenhagen Vase 59–60
Corinth 78
critical heritage studies 4, 6–7
curriculum 10, 18, 25, 34–35, 39

Danish, culture 26, 28, 52, 57, 103;
    Danishness 27; People's Party 4, 104
Delos 78
Delphi 78–79
democracy 1, 8, 18, 25, 38, 57, 61, 102
Díaz-Andreu, Margarita 13, 78
Due, Otto Steen 30

Edda 3, 11
Egyptology 41
Eleusis 85
Erechtheion 88
Etruscan 54–55, 66–67, 70–71, 73
Euripides 19, 30–33
European, citizens 4; culture 11, 16–19,
    29, 37–38, 40–42, 53, 80, 104; identity
    1, 4, 10–11, 57, 73, 81, 100–102, 103
European Heritage Label 1–3, 11,
    18–19, 57, 100

European Monetary Union 4, 40
European Union (EU) 1, 4, 39–40, 43,
    100, 104
Exner, Johannes 95

Fisherman of Halikarnassos 85–87, 97
Folk High School 15
Frederik III (King of Denmark and
    Norway) 51
Frederiksborg Castle (Museum of
    National History) 12, 15
French Revolution 2
Freund, H.E. 71
Friborg, Flemming 64, 66

Germany 3, 14, 16, 27, 29, 55, 80, 84
Gertz, Martin Clarentius 29–30, 44
globalisation 72, 104–105
Glyptothek (Munich) 47, 61
Goethe, Johann Wolfgang von 23
Golden Dawn 3
Goldhill, Simon 37
Gothic 11
Greece 1, 3, 14, 25, 29, 46–49, 51, 53,
    55, 57, 62, 67–68, 70–71, 79, 81, 87,
    89, 103; Bronze Age 53
Greek, culture 17, 20–21, 24, 28, 30,
    36–37, 39–42, 53, 55, 57, 72, 103
Grundtvig, Nikolaj Frederik Severin
    15, 27, 39, 52
gymnasium 21, 29

Halikarnassos *see* Bodrum
Hama 51, 59, 81
Hansen, Christian and Theophilus 13
Hartmann, Moritz 9
Hauge, Hans 36, 43
Helbig, Wolfgang 66, 67
Hellenisation 16
Hellenism 25, 38–39, 43, 103
Herder, Johann Gottfried 15, 23,
    27, 37
Hesiod 33
Homer 29–30, 33–34, 87, 103
House of European History 1
humanists 2, 25–26, 29, 46–47
Humboldt, Alexander von 23–24, 29

identity(ies) *see* European
imagined communities 8, 39, 50

imagined geography 4, 6–10, 12–13,
    17–18, 21, 24, 28, 37, 43, 45–46, 48,
    58, 64, 73–74, 76, 80, 95, 98, 100,
    102, 104–105
imperialism 3, 37, 78
Italy 3, 11, 38, 46–47, 50, 55,
    80–81, 92

Jacobsen, Carl 16, 61–62, 66
Jacobsen, J.C. 15–16
Jeppesen, Kristian 18, 76–96, 98–99

Kalydon 81
Kinch, Karl Frederik 81
Krischen, Fritz 90
Kunstkammer 51, 79

Lange, Thor 30
Late Antiquity 55, 97–98
Latin 13, 20, 23–30, 34, 37, 39, 41,
    43–44, 79, 81, 88–89
Lindos 16, 80–81, 85, 93, 102
Louvre 16, 48, 51, 59, 62, 74
Lowenthal, David 98

Maastrict Treaty 4
Macdonald, Sharon 6
Macron, Emmanuel 1, 3, 8, 19
Madvig, Johan Nicolai 25–27, 29
Magna Graecia 55
Marchand, Suzanne 14, 16
Martindale, Charles 5
Menander 33
Meyer, Jørgen 39
Møller, Niels 30
Müller, Carl Ludvig 52
Müller, Sophus 52
multiculturalism 42, 72, 101, 104
Museum of Underwater Archaeology
    87, 96

Napoleon 14, 23
National Exhibition (Aarhus 1909)
    76–77
National Gallery (Copenhagen) 50
nationalism 4, 8, 13–15, 35, 50–51,
    78, 86
National Museum (Copenhagen) 9, 14,
    17, 45, 50–59, 61, 67, 73, 79, 89,
    100–102

Nielsen, Valdemar 33
Nordic, mythology 41
Norse, Old 26–28
Ny Carlsberg Glyptotek 16–87, 45, 50,
    59–74, 76, 79, 102

Obama, Barack 1, 8
Oldtidskundskab 16, 18, 20–44, 73, 102
Olympia 78–79
Orientalism 7
Ørsted, Hans Christian 25
Østergaard, Uffe 15
Ottoman Empire 80, 83, 85, 96

Parthenon 8–9, 45, 51, 55, 59, 84, 88
Pedersen, Poul 96–97
philhellenism 14
Piraeus 85
place-making 10
Plato 25, 29, 34, 37, 103
Poulsen, Birte 96
public schools 13

Reformation 11
Renaissance 2–3, 5–6, 11, 24, 28–29,
    38, 41–42, 46, 53, 62, 96
Roman, culture 6, 21, 26, 34, 39–40,
    43, 47–48, 57; anti-Romanism 39;
    Empire, fall of 53
Rome 13, 24, 76, 78, 81, 93, 99, 101,
    104; Capitoline Museums 46, 74
Rousseau, Jean-Jacques 36
Royal Art Academy 13
Royal Danish Academy of Fine Arts 84
Royal Danish Academy of Sciences
    and Letters 16

Said, Edward 7
Schmidt, Helle Thorning 100
Simonsen, Lauritz Vedel 51
Snorri Sturluson 3
Soane, John 92–93
Socrates 34, 100–101
Sophocles 30–33
Sparta 33
Syria 51, 81

Thomsen, Christian Jürgensen 17,
    50, 80
Thomsen, Ole 42
Thorvaldsen, Bertel 13, 52, 61
Thorvaldsens Museum 50, 74–75
Trojan kings 3
Turkey 17–18, 47–48, 76–99, 103–104

united Left party 15
University of Copenhagen 25, 27, 30,
    40, 79, 84
Ussing, Johannes Ludovicus 79–80

Vienna 13, 45, 59

Wiedewelt, Johannes 13
Winckelmann, Johann Joachim 13, 24,
    47, 52
Wivel, Peter 38
Wolf, Christa 38
Wolf, Friedrich August 23
World War I 2, 81, 85
World War II 1
Worsaae, Jens Jacob Asmussen 14, 80

Xenophon 33

For Product Safety Concerns and Information please contact our EU
representative GPSR@taylorandfrancis.com Taylor & Francis Verlag GmbH,
Kaufingerstraße 24, 80331 München, Germany

Batch number: 08153772

Printed by Printforce, the Netherlands